On This Day In

CHICAGO HISTORY

JOHN R. SCHMIDT

Charleston ⊣⊢ London

THE
History
PRESS

Published by The History Press
Charleston, SC 29403
www.historypress.net

Front cover, row 1, right: Wrigley Building postcard, *author's collection. Front cover, row 3, right*: State Street at night, *photo by the author. Back cover, top*: Water Tower postcard, *author's collection.*

First published 2014

Manufactured in the United States

ISBN 978.1.62619.253.9

Library of Congress CIP data applied for.

CONTENTS

Acknowledgements	5
Introduction	7
1. January	9
2. February	40
3. March	70
4. April	102
5. May	132
6. June	166
7. July	196
8. August	227
9. September	260
10. October	290
11. November	322
12. December	352
About the Author	384

ACKNOWLEDGEMENTS

Newspapers are the rough drafts of history. Most of this book was based on contemporary newspaper stories. Thank you to Ray Gadke at the Regenstein Library (University of Chicago) and to the staff at the Harold Washington Library in Chicago, who helped me locate those rough drafts. And thank you to the people who first wrote them.

After twenty-five years, I again have the opportunity to dedicate a book to my wife, Terri—so I do, with all my love, admiration and gratitude. Thank you to my son, Nicholas Schmidt, who has carried on the family interest in history, after listening to me talk about it for thirty years. Finally, thank you to my daughter, Tracy Samantha Schmidt, whose personal example and professional contacts got me back to writing history.

A.M.D.G.

INTRODUCTION

This is not a grand overview of Chicago history. Rather, it's 366 snapshots, taken at different times. Put them together, and you have a portrait of Chicago.

(And let's clear up something right at the start. In this book, when I say "Chicago," I mean the city *and* the suburbs *and* the exurbs. Leave the political boundaries to the politicians.)

There's a bit of everything here. Because this is Chicago, you will find politics. Crime, too. Read some stories, and you'll marvel at how things have changed—can you imagine anyone in 2014 trying to protect valuables by inscribing them with a social security number? You'll also find that Chicagoans of a century ago had many of the same issues as the people of today.

The 366 stories don't all carry the same weight. Some are more historically important than others. Because of the format, certain events had to be left out. On August

15, 1812, Fort Dearborn was destroyed. Exactly 155 years later, the Picasso sculpture was unveiled in the Loop. One of these stories had to go. If you wish, take a moment now and see which one I decided to keep.

Okay, you're back. Hopefully, you skimmed a few more dates before you remembered you had been reading the introduction. But I'm through here anyway, so feel free to dive back into the book.

Welcome to the history of Chicago—because there's more to it than just a fire.

January 1, 1951

Bushman, lord of Lincoln Park Zoo.
Author's collection.

Time magazine had called him "the best known and most popular civic figure in Chicago." Now he was dead, and the city mourned Bushman, the Lincoln Park Zoo's gorilla. For twenty years, he'd entertained visitors. Though he generally had a sunny disposition, like any celebrity, Bushman occasionally lost patience with the paparazzi, and sometimes he'd throw food at photographers. When he suffered a heart attack last summer, over a quarter million people filed silently past his cage in a single week. Today, a second heart attack claimed his life, at age twenty-two.

January 2, 1900

Yes, the Chicago River really does flow backward. The river's natural course emptied into Lake Michigan, and that dumped all the wastes of civilization into the city's drinking water. On paper, the way to stop this was simple, and had two parts: (1) Put a barrier between the Chicago River and Lake Michigan. (2) Connect the Chicago River to the Des Plaines River system, which flowed southwest toward the Gulf of Mexico. Building the barrier between river and lake was the easy part. Connecting the two river systems meant dredging the twenty-eight-mile-long Chicago Drainage Canal, a task that took seven years and was called the greatest public works project in history. As the canal neared completion, St. Louis realized it would soon be getting drinking water flavored with Chicago sewage and prepared a lawsuit to halt the project. Rather than wait to stage an elaborate dedication ceremony, Chicago officials simply opened the sluice gates on January 2, 1900. The Chicago River began flowing backward, which it has done ever since.

January 3, 1936

Dr. Silber Peacock, a prominent Edgewater pediatrician, was found brutally murdered in his Cadillac along a lonely stretch of Francisco Avenue today. The doctor had been summoned by phone to treat a sick child, and his wife thought him the victim of a robbery gone wrong. But that wasn't good enough for the local papers. Over the next months, they went wild with speculation. Had Dr. Peacock been having an affair and been killed by his lover? Had the lover's husband killed him? Had he botched an abortion and been killed in retribution? Had he been selling drugs and been knocked off by rival pushers? In the end, it turned out Dr. Peacock really had been the victim of a robbery gone wrong, which had netted the perps all of twenty dollars. And shortly after the two killers were sentenced to long prison terms, Mrs. Peacock gave birth to the doctor's posthumous daughter.

January 4, 1968

Mercy Hospital had stood at 25th and Prairie since 1869. A block away, a $26 million replacement facility was now ready and waiting. At eight o'clock this morning, with temperatures near zero and snow piled on the ground, hospital workers began the delicate task of moving 160 patients from the old building to the new one. The Metropolitan Ambulance Association had provided twenty vehicles without charge. One by one, patients were bundled onto stretchers and shuttled over. Meanwhile, office staff walked the thousands of medical folders through the bone-chilling cold to the new Mercy. Everyone seemed in good spirits. By 4:00 p.m., the transfer was complete.

January 5, 1968

Today, Chicago got its first in-city ski resort. Thunder Mountain, located on the site of the Carey Brickyard at 2600 North Narragansett Avenue, boasted a 285-foot vertical drop from the top of its man-made hill. Two ski instructors were already on the premises, and a former brick kiln was being converted into a chalet. Though a toboggan run and a 125-room motel were also planned, Thunder Mountain ran into warm winters and public indifference, closing after two seasons.

January 6, 1960

Smell-O-Vision. The word sounded like a joke, and it had been used that way in a 1944 Bugs Bunny cartoon. Yet now it was really here in Chicago, courtesy of Mike Todd Jr. The occasion was the world premiere of Todd's new movie, *Scent of Mystery*. The motion picture industry had been answering the challenge of TV with various gimmicks, such as 3-D and extra-wide screens. Smell-O-Vision was the latest. During the course of the movie, cues on the soundtrack would cause the release of various odors into the theater, which were supposed to advance the plot. *Scent of Mystery* starred Denholm Elliott and Peter Lorre in an otherwise-routine thriller. Todd went all-out for the Cinestage premiere, with music, searchlights and a personal appearance from megastar Elizabeth Taylor, his father's widow. However, technical problems kept the Smell-O-Vision system from working properly. By the time all the kinks were ironed out, poor word of mouth killed the movie's chances. Competition from a similar cinema-odor system called AromaRama didn't help. Todd's movie was later rereleased under the title *Holiday in Spain*—without the Smell-O-Vision.

January 7, 1942

One month had passed since the Japanese attacked Pearl Harbor and plunged America into World War II. Rubber was being rationed, which meant tire shortages—which meant tire theft. The latest Chicago incident took place at North Side Tire on Ashland Avenue, where thieves made off with twenty tires, twenty batteries and the company truck. Meanwhile, tire dealers on the outer fringes of the city were complaining that the local rationing board was favoring dealers located closer to downtown. In Springfield, laws were being prepared to prevent price gouging. However, the lawmakers seemed more concerned that fewer tire sales would mean less tax revenue. And who knew how much longer the war would last?

January 8, 1901

The big sporting news in Chicago today was the opening of the first national bowling championships. The American Bowling Congress Tournament was being contested on six specially built lanes in the Wellsbach Building on Wabash Avenue. The three-day event attracted two hundred bowlers from various cities who competed in three events—Team, Doubles and Singles. The most publicized bowler was Cap Anson, the star first baseman who'd recently retired from the diamond. But when all the pins had been toppled, a one-time journeyman pitcher named Frank Brill had captured the Singles event and, with it, the gold medal proclaiming him the first National Champion Bowler.

Opening squad in the American Bowling Congress Tournament. *From* Chicago Record, *January 9, 1901.*

January 9, 1924

Chicago had four companies operating elevated railroads. Today, Samuel Insull and a group of financiers consolidated three of the roads under a holding company known as Chicago Rapid Transit. The Metropolitan, which operated the Garfield Park trunk line and its branches, was the most expensive acquisition, pegged at $16.1 million. The South Side L was valued at $10.3 million, while the Northwestern carried a list price of $9.9 million. Though the Oak Park Elevated (Lake Street) was still independent, Insull's group expected to acquire the line at a receiver's sale during the next fortnight. The new CRT promised to give the city more efficient L service while maintaining the current seven-cent fare. Future extensions of existing lines were already under discussion.

January 10, 1910

The First National Bank of Englewood, at 349 West 63rd Street, added five hundred new depositors in the past month. The head cashier credited an article recently published in the bank's monthly magazine, *Savings*. The article told of a local housewife who waited until her husband fell asleep each evening, then went through his pants' pockets and collected all the loose change, which she'd deposit in the bank the next morning. All the other Englewood housewives interviewed seemed happy with this new plan for saving, and many of the husbands said they were happy as well. The First National Bank of Englewood certainly was happy.

January 11, 1984

Mike Royko began writing for the *Chicago Daily News* in 1963, moving over to the *Sun-Times* when the *News* folded. He won a Pulitzer Prize and became one of the country's favorite syndicated columnists. In November 1983, Rupert Murdoch bought the *Sun-Times*. Royko didn't like Murdoch's style of journalism, saying that "no self-respecting fish" would be wrapped in a Murdoch paper. On this January 11, Royko signed on at the *Tribune*. His first column celebrated the superiority of sitting, as opposed to standing. Over at the *Sun-Times*, Royko's former paper refused to admit he'd jumped ship. It continued reprinting his old columns, so now Chicago newspaper readers awoke each morning to the joy of dueling Roykos. The *Sun-Times* also tried to force the columnist to come back by taking him to court. Judge Anthony Scotillo dismissed the suit, and the *Sun-Times* dropped the matter. Royko remained at the *Tribune* until his death in 1997.

January 12, 1966

By 1966, O'Hare was already the world's busiest airport. But those were simpler times, and policing O'Hare was simpler, too. The airport was patrolled by fifty-two Chicago policemen. Most of the property was unfenced, so the cops had to intercept cars that blundered onto back roads dangerously close to runways. The FBI, U.S. Customs and the Secret Service all had personnel at O'Hare. However, there were no security checkpoints. Anyone could wander through the terminal, right up to the boarding gates. Groups of teens often showed up on weekends, just to hang out and watch the planes take off. No one seemed to mind that rifle-toting hunters stalked animals in the wooded areas at the southwest corner. In the summer, children were often seen swimming in one of the airport ponds. Simpler times, indeed!

January 13, 1834

The young New York writer Charles Fenno Hoffman was traveling through the wilds of the Midwest in search of adventure. On this date, he was stopping at the Fort Dearborn garrison. His hosts took him along on a hunt for a gray wolf that was attacking livestock, and Hoffman later described the day's events in his book *A Winter in the West*. This volume was one of the first to acquaint readers in the rest of the country with the brand-new town named Chicago. Hoffman himself became a celebrated poet, but he suffered a nervous breakdown and spent the last thirty-five years of his life in asylums.

Chicago around the time of Charles Fenno Hoffman's visit.
Author's collection.

January 14, 1927

The No Jury Art Exhibit was being held at Marshall Field's this morning when two women from the Illinois Vigilance Society arrived. The ladies were particularly interested in six nude paintings. After taking down notes, they left to visit Police Chief Morgan Collins. A few hours later, two policewomen showed up at the exhibit. They also inspected the six nudes, checking them against the notes made by the Vigilance Society ladies. The policewomen then called on the director of Field's art galleries and told him those paintings would have to go. He protested that other art shows featured nude works. The policewomen remained resolute. A workman was summoned and began taking down "A Dancing Figure," "Sin or Religion" and the other paintings in question. "Somebody might let the patrons know about this," he mumbled. "Anyway, they left a lot of them here."

January 15, 1925

Sometimes it takes an outsider to present a fresh perspective. When the respected French author Abbé Ernest Dimnet visited Chicago on a lecture tour, he was asked for his views on how to solve the city's bootlegging crime problem. The good father responded that Chicago needed a guillotine! "In France we would be horrified at such a crime wave that has deluged dry Chicago," he said. "However, there is something in the utter finality of the descending blade of a guillotine that inspires a healthy respect for the law." Dimnet added that the executions must be public and suggested that Grant Park would be a suitable place for the Municipal Razor. The city eventually put Buckingham Fountain on the site instead.

January 16, 1997

The Chicago Public Library confirmed the story—its free Internet service had been cut off because the library hadn't paid its bills. The previous March, Bill Gates had given the system $1 million in software, licensing rights and other equipment, with the idea of extending Internet access to all eighty-one library branches. Yet nearly a year later, free public Internet was available only at the downtown library, the two regionals and four branches. And during the last two weeks, patrons at these locations had found the terminals decorated with signs reading "Out of Order" or "Under Construction." The president of MCS Net, the Internet provider, said his company had tried to work with the library on a payment plan, even granting a sixty-day extension. The monthly charge was $200, plus "very substantial overtime usage." The Internet service had shut down automatically when the bills weren't paid. Today, a library official hand-carried a check to MCS Net to settle the deadbeat account. There was no immediate word when the library's Internet service would be restored.

January 17, 1923

The "auto vamp" was an attractive young woman who'd been hitching rides from men along the city's boulevards, then blackmailing them by threatening to tell their wives. The previous August, police had arrested twenty-one-year-old Jeane Miller as the vamp. She had skipped bail. On this evening, an insurance adjuster recognized the woman on Oak Street. Deciding to make a citizen's arrest, he grabbed Miller by the arm and told her to get into his car. Meanwhile, a second man happened along, thought the lady was being kidnapped and wrestled her away. The two of them roared away in the man's car, the adjuster chasing after them in his own car. A motorcycle cop saw the speeding cars and took off after them down Oak Street. At Lake Shore Drive, both cars halted and the two drivers jumped out, intent on settling things man-to-man. The cop pushed through the gathering crowd. He calmed everyone down, saying that the matter would be sorted out at the police station. There, Miller was placed under arrest for bond forfeiture. The two men swore out complaints against each other. The reign of the auto vamp seemed to be over.

January 18, 1952

Today, Chicagoans learned the reason their meat tasted different lately—they may have been eating horse meat. Federal investigators had been probing a packing plant in Lake Zurich. The feds claimed that the "pure beef" shipped from there was actually 40 percent horse, with most of it winding up in city supermarkets. The Chicago mob was thought to be behind the scheme—there was a nice profit available, since beef cost fifty-nine cents per pound versus fourteen cents per pound for horse meat. During the next few months, hamburger sales dropped by over 50 percent, and some prominent restaurants were temporarily shut down. But in the end, only a few people served some short jail time, and meat consumption rebounded.

January 19, 1935

Marshall Field's State Street store introduced a new garment called the jockey brief today. Manufactured by Coopers, the innovative style of men's underwear did away with leg sections and featured a front pouch for extra support where it was most needed. The store's complete stock of six hundred packages was gone by noon. Field's sold an additional twelve thousand units within the next few weeks, and soon, the briefs were being marketed throughout the country.

January 20, 1985

At 6:18 a.m., the temperature at O'Hare was officially recorded as negative twenty-seven degrees. That made this day the coldest in the history of Chicago. Since the previous record of negative twenty-six degrees had been posted only three years ago, there was speculation the Earth was moving into a new ice age. Fortunately, it was a Sunday, and most Chicagoans had the luxury of staying home. And when the mercury rose to a balmy negative eight the next day, there was also the consolation that spring was only two months away.

January 21, 1937

Movie star Katharine Hepburn was appearing in the play *Jane Eyre* at a Loop theater. She was staying at the Ambassador East. Then, millionaire aviator Howard Hughes arrived in town and checked into the same hotel. Hepburn and Hughes had been an item for months. Word spread that a Windy City wedding was in the works. When the County Building opened for business on the morning of January 21, thousands of celebrity-watchers surged through the doors, hoping to see the happy couple get hitched. County Clerk Michael Flynn helped the story along by announcing he was ready to personally issue a marriage license to Katie and Howard. By midday, over three thousand people clogged the building's corridors, including many county employees who'd abandon their posts to join the stakeout. Ordinary couples trying to get their own marriage licenses had trouble getting through the mob. Closing time came, but still no Hepburn-Hughes. That evening, and for a few days afterward, reporters followed Hepburn back and forth to the theater, with no result. Hughes remained in the hotel. In the end, Katharine Hepburn and Howard Hughes never did get married, in Chicago or anyplace else.

January 22, 1988

Chicago public school officials were wondering, where did their students go? The past October 30, when the official school census was taken, the number of students was pegged at 419,537, a drop of about 11,000 from the previous school year. However, the enrollment at Catholic schools was also down. The CPS demographer speculated that most of the missing students had transferred to suburban public schools. It was also possible that some of the students were from Mexican families who'd returned to their homeland because they couldn't find work in Chicago. The demographer dismissed the notion that enrollment was down because students were dropping out—after all, the elementary schools were losing students faster than the high schools. A CPS spokesman suggested that school reforms now under discussion might reverse the slide. What remained to be seen was "whether parents will feel the changes made will make enough of a positive impact to bring students back."

January 23, 1969

A bit of local wisdom says that Chicago has two seasons—winter and road construction. On this particular winter day, motorists on 31st Boulevard were hoping the other season would hurry up and get here. The problem was potholes. A half-mile stretch of roadway between California and Western was pitted and scarred like the surface of the moon. Though the potholes didn't have names like the lunar craters, daily commuters were all too familiar with the situation. Most of them knew the course, managing to safely navigate with judicious swerving. Every so often, though, the potholes would claim another victim. Then it was time to get the spare out of the trunk and change the blown tire, in typical single-digit January temperature. Drivers who merely lost a hubcap to a pothole didn't even bother to stop. A *Sun-Times* reporter sent to investigate the carnage measured the biggest hole as three feet wide, four feet long and just under two feet deep. When informed of the situation on 31st Boulevard, the city's streets and sanitation commissioner promised the paper that the road would be fixed by the next morning.

January 24, 1972

In May 1889, three years after the Haymarket Riot, the city erected a monument honoring the policemen killed in the incident. The statue of a uniformed police captain was placed in Haymarket Square. The inscription on the base read, "In the name of the people of Illinois, I command peace." For a time, the statue was moved to Union Park, before being brought back to Haymarket during the 1950s. Beginning in 1968, the Haymarket Cop became the focus of protest. On the riot anniversary that year, vandals smeared it with paint. The next year, the radical Weatherman group blew it up. A new statue was erected and blown up again. The statue was again replaced, this time with a twenty-four-hour police guard. By 1972, the city concluded that symbolism had been satisfied. On January 24, it was announced that the statue's new home would be police headquarters, at 11th and State. Some years later, it was moved to the courtyard of the Police Training Academy. Since 2007, the Haymarket Cop has resided at the new Central Police Headquarters at 3510 South Michigan Avenue.

January 25, 1931

Paul Newman played a Chicago con man in 1973's best picture, *The Sting*. Newman's character was based on a real person, Joseph Weil, aka the Yellow Kid. On this day in 1931, Weil was in Chicago police custody, charged with bilking a Michigan man out of $15,000 in a mining deal. When the cops took the opportunity to parade him through a police lineup, the Kid objected. "Sure I'm a con man—the best," he told a *Tribune* reporter. "But I've always taken from those who could afford the education." He wasn't a hypocrite who robbed the poor and then sat in a church pew on Sunday. Besides, the Chicago cops were treating him shamefully. "Yesterday they exhibited me to a farmer who lost two cases of eggs," the Kid complained. "The value was $8.50. I have never been so humiliated." His chat with the reporter over, the Kid was taken back to his cell. He beat this particular rap and continued his career until old age finally caught up with him. Yellow Kid Joseph Weil died in 1976 at the age of ninety-nine. Whether he ever saw *The Sting* is not known.

January 26, 1986

Coach Mike Ditka's 1985 Chicago Bears had the strongest defense in football. In Walter Payton, they had an all-time great running back. In Jim McMahon, they had their sharpest quarterback in twenty years. They also had William Perry, aka the Refrigerator, a 335-pound rookie defensive tackle who'd scored three touchdowns as an occasional goal-line plunger. The team went 15-1 in the regular season. But when they cut a rap record titled "The Super Bowl Shuffle," superstitious Chicagoans felt the Bears were arrogantly tempting fate. This time, jinxes didn't matter. The team ripped through the playoffs without breaking a sweat. On January 26, 1986, the super Bears blew away the New England Patriots in Super Bowl XX, 46–10. Was a dynasty in the making?

January 27, 1967

Chicago's worst snowstorm began about 5:00 a.m. on January 26, 1967. At first, it seemed like any other January storm. But it wouldn't stop. In the early afternoon, some businesses started closing up and letting staff go home early. By the evening rush hour, things were really bad. The plows couldn't keep up with the continuing snow. Traffic came to a standstill. Even the L stopped. After a few hours of not moving, people simply left their cars where they were and started walking. People stuck downtown checked into hotels or camped out in the lobby when all the rooms were filled. The snow continued all night, until 10:00 a.m. on January 27. Then it stopped. Chicago's blizzard of '67 had dumped twenty-three inches of snow on the ground in twenty-nine hours, a record for the rate of snowfall. Over twenty thousand vehicles had been abandoned. And within the next ten days, two more storms piled up an additional fourteen inches of snow. Yeah, those kids in 2014 don't know what a *real* blizzard is…

January 28, 1974

A group of aldermen was asking the city council to repeal various obsolete laws. The local statute banning female bartenders had been declared unconstitutional some years earlier, but it was still on the books. Another law said that only the U.S. flag, state flags or the flags of friendly nations could be publicly displayed, which meant that waving a Cubs or Sox pennant was technically illegal. Likewise, motorists on lower Wacker Drive were violating a ban on driving a vehicle through a tunnel under a city street. The city law against flag-pole sitting was so broadly written that a child might be arrested for climbing a tree. One of the aldermen said their move to get rid of the dead-letter laws was "our contribution to the grand old tradition of spring cleaning."

January 29, 1857

On this date, a man named James Hollingworth ran an ad in the *Tribune* announcing he was prepared to move or raise your building. In 1857 Chicago, that was a booming business. Officials had decided it was time for the central business district to have a sewer system. Rather than abandon the current site and start over on higher ground, the plan was to jack up all the buildings where they were. Some buildings were raised as much as fourteen feet. When a building reached the desired height, a new foundation was put under it. Then a sewer was constructed along the top of the old street. Next the sewer was covered over and land filled in to meet the new building level. The final step was paving the street on top of the fill. This procedure would go on at hundreds of different sites for nearly twenty years. But in the end, Chicago had the most modern sewer system in the world, and public health was much better.

January 30, 1904

President William Rainey Harper was talking to graduate students at the University of Chicago about the ideal college professor. Harper said that a professor should be married, have at least three children, identify with a church and take an active interest in public affairs. If a professor was younger than forty, he was also expected to hold a PhD. Harper thought that professors should use their summer months for additional study. "That is what summer vacation is for," he said. "The reason that American scholarship has not advanced more in comparison with Germany and other countries is that our professors think they need four months of rest."

William Rainey Harper's University of Chicago. *Author's collection.*

January 31, 1963

A new map released by the Chicago Commission on Human Relations highlighted the locations of four growing minorities—Mexican, Puerto Rican, "Oriental" and "Southern White." The largest of these groups was Mexicans, defined as persons born in Mexico or having at least one relative living in Mexico. The most recent census had counted about forty-five thousand Mexicans in Chicago, most residing on the West Side or in the long-established South Chicago community. The other Spanish-speaking group, Puerto Ricans, numbered thirty-two thousand. They were scattered throughout the city. The twenty-five thousand in the "Oriental" category included such different peoples as Chinese, Japanese, Filipinos and American Indians. Aside from the five thousand Chinese living in the city's traditional Chinatown, there was no large concentration of Asians in any one place. The twenty-five thousand "Southern Whites" included many new arrivals, most of them settled in Uptown and Lincoln Park. The commission was sending the map and statistical analysis to six thousand professionals doing work in ethnic demographics.

February 1, 1920

Edward F. Cullerton, dean of the city council, died at his home at 1632 West 20th Street today. He was seventy-eight years old. Cullerton had dropped out of elementary school to work as a canalboat driver, and eventually he drifted into Democratic politics. He was first elected to the city council in 1871. He stayed there for the rest of his life, except for a two-year interval when the reformers managed to oust him. Known as Foxy Ed, Cullerton was shrewd and silent. The clean government crowd despised him, the voters of his ward loved him. "I make no pre-election promises," he said in a rare campaign speech. "I judge each ordinance or resolution when it comes up, and in the light of the circumstances that then exist." Soon after the alderman's death, the city renamed 20th Street as Cullerton Street. And in 2014—over 140 years after Foxy Ed's first election victory—members of the Cullerton clan still play a powerful role in Chicago politics.

February 2, 1977

Today, Chicagoans read the latest news about Warren Park. In 1965, the Edgewater Country Club began negotiations to sell its property at Western and Pratt. Developers planned to build high-rises on the site. Community opposition exploded, and the state purchased the land for use as Warren Park in 1969. Six years later, the state transferred the property to the Chicago Park District. Now the Park District's plans were coming under fire. A new nine-hole golf course was to be included in Warren Park, and some people didn't like that. The Park District compromised by chopping about 10 percent off the planned golf acreage. However, revenue from golfers was going to be used to finance the rest of the park's $11 million price tag, so the course had to stay. Despite the latest protests, the plan went forward. Warren Park was finally finished, and green fees at its Robert Black Golf Course continue to pay for other recreational projects.

February 3, 1986

Hopes had been high when Old Chicago opened in Bolingbrook in 1975. The concept was daring—build an amusement park, surround it with stores and put the whole thing indoors. Investors had tripped over one another racing forward with seed money. When finished, the complex enclosed eleven acres. The amusement park had thirty-one rides, including a roller coaster, a Ferris wheel and the old Riverview favorite, the Rotor. Shopping was available in over one hundred specialty stores. Circus acts and a Dixieland band provided entertainment. Opening day attendance was fifteen thousand, and during the first few months, massive traffic jams backed up the interstate. After the initial curiosity wore off, patronage declined. The huge Great America amusement park in Gurnee opened in 1976 and lured away many customers. Stores began leaving. The whole thing closed in 1980. There followed years of discussion on whether anything could be done to resurrect some of the shopping mall. Nothing seemed feasible, and the wreckers began tearing down Old Chicago on February 3, 1986.

February 4, 1977

It was a frigid Friday evening rush hour, getting on toward 5:30 p.m. A northbound Lake-Ryan L train had just stopped at the Randolph-Wabash station. Now the motorman started up and moved around the curve from Wabash onto Lake. Up ahead, a Ravenswood train was stopped on the tracks. The trailing Lake-Ryan train came around the curve at a sedate fifteen miles per hour. Then, for whatever reason, it kept going, crashing into the rear of the parked Ravenswood train. The impact knocked the first three cars of the Lake-Ryan train off the track, and they fell to the street below. The No. 4 car also derailed, hanging over the edge of the L structure. Police and firemen soon arrived on the scene. Rescue efforts went on for hours. Nearby stores and restaurants were turned into emergency rooms. Later, an official investigation attributed the crash to motorman error. Eleven people were killed and 180 injured, making this the deadliest accident in Chicago L history.

February 5, 1923

Emile Coue was coming to Chicago! The French "Miracle Man" was promoting a self-help technique called autosuggestion. Repeat the simple phrase "Day by day, in every way, I am getting better and better" and your unconscious would eventually do the rest. Coue's lectures at Orchestra Hall drew packed houses. At the conclusion of his final session, he even got five people to throw away their crutches and walk. Coue denied he was a healer but said he was only a teacher who'd shown these people how to overcome their "psychic paralysis." The Miracle Man's ideas of positive thinking later inspired such later luminaries as Norman Vincent Peale and W. Clement Stone. Still, it's worth noting that the February 5 *Tribune* announcement of Coue's Chicago lectures appeared on the Entertainment page—just below the ad for the Four Marx Brothers.

February 6, 1951

Paul Harvey, the young ABC radio newscaster, had been told security was lax at the top-secret Argonne National Laboratory, west of the city. Taking along two whistle-blowers, Harvey drove out to investigate. They arrived at the facility shortly after midnight. Harvey scaled the chain-link fence, dropped onto the grounds and was immediately caught by a guard. Because his driver's license was in his birth name—Paul Aurandt—at first it was thought the intruder might be an atomic spy. After questioning by the FBI, Harvey was released. The U.S. attorney brought charges against the newsman, but the grand jury refused to indict. Depending on which side of the political fence you were on, either (A) President Truman was out to get the conservative commentator or (B) FBI chief J. Edgar Hoover was protecting Harvey. In any event, throughout the rest of his long career, Paul Harvey made sure to stay on the proper side of the fence at government facilities.

February 7, 1895

St. Hedwig parish had been founded to serve Polish Catholics in Bucktown. As 1895 began, the parish was engulfed in a civil war. One side supported the pastor, Reverend Joseph Barzynski. The other side rallied around assistant pastor Reverend Anthony Kozlowski, saying they wanted the laity to have a greater role in running the parish. First there were protests against the pastor at Sunday Mass. Then, on the evening of February 7, about three thousand people tried to storm the rectory, where Barzynski and another assistant were holed up. When the first police arrived, some of the women in the crowd threw red pepper into the cops' eyes, and a second squad had to be summoned to disperse the rioters. Some months later, Kozlowski and his supporters left the Roman Catholic Church. They affiliated with the Old Catholic Church, now known as the Polish National Catholic Church.

February 8, 1951

The temperature had dropped to negative eleven in the early morning hours when two policemen found a frozen body in the gangway at 3108 South Vernon Avenue. The body was that of a young woman. Later she would be identified as Dorothy Mae Stevens, age twenty-three. The two cops bundled her in blankets and took her to Michael Reese Hospital for a postmortem. At the hospital, one of the staff heard a groan—Stevens was alive! Her body temperature had dropped to sixty-four degrees, she was breathing at four breaths a minute and her blood pressure was zero. The doctors weren't sure what to do. They decided to give Stevens blood plasma and a cortisone shot and put her in a refrigerated room to thaw out. By evening she had recovered enough to tell her story. She'd been drinking all day, had passed out, then lay in the gangway for eight hours. The booze in her system had evidently acted like anti-freeze. Stevens lost nine of her fingers and had to have both legs amputated. By the time she was released from the hospital in June, she was able to joke, "I'll never be able to eat frozen food again."

February 9, 1971

A controversial towing service was becoming a hot-button issue in the Forty-fourth Ward aldermanic race. North Siders had been complaining about Lincoln Towing for years. The company was accused of towing legally parked cars, then charging exorbitant rates to recover them—$28 a tow, more than double what other companies charged. People who complained were insulted or threatened. One suburban man had recently been awarded $34,000 in damages after a knife attack by a Lincoln employee. On this date, aldermanic candidate Richard Simpson filed a $1 million class-action lawsuit in Circuit Court, saying the company was "endangering and menacing" area residents. The publicity from the suit was only one factor enabling reformer Simpson to gain an upset victory in the April aldermanic election. The next year, Steve Goodman's song "The Lincoln Park Pirates" further damaged Lincoln's reputation. The city finally passed new laws regulating towing services, and the reign of terror was over.

February 10, 1916

George Mundelein had arrived in Chicago as the new Catholic archbishop. The leaders of the city and state were giving him a welcoming banquet at the University Club. During the first course, one of the guests felt faint, got up from his chair, then collapsed. Other people began complaining of upset stomachs. The banquet went on, though more guests became ill, and those who weren't stopped eating. Doctors thought the bouillon in the soup might have spoiled. A closer examination revealed that the soup had been laced with arsenic. Suspicion fell on a cook named Jean Crones, who had disappeared. A search of the man's apartment revealed numerous phials of poison and piles of anarchist literature. All the poison victims recovered. Jean Crones turned out to be an Italian radical named Nestor Dondoglio. He was never caught.

February 11, 1906

Today, Chicagoans learned their city had the most dangerous police district in the world. The *Tribune* devoted two full pages to the saga of "Bloody Maxwell," the area

between Harrison and Sixteenth, from the river west to Wood Street. The Twenty-first District police station at 943 West Maxwell Street was like a Wild West fort surrounded by hostile Indians. The area was filled with recent immigrants—Irish, Germans, Poles, Italians, Greeks, Russians, Jews and others—all thrown uneasily together in crowded, dirty tenements. They lived "more like beasts than human beings" and many turned to crime. There wasn't enough police manpower to patrol the area, and the thugs knew it. Even the bravest cop would never enter a building alone. So it was in 1906. Over a century later, most of the old Twenty-first District is gentrified or part of the UIC campus.

"Bloody Maxwell." *Author's collection.*

February 12, 1909

This was the 100th anniversary of Abraham Lincoln's birth, with celebrations throughout the nation. Here in Chicago, in Lincoln's home state, the festivities were elaborate. The day was declared a holiday. Schools and government offices closed, and most businesses also shut down. At 10:00 a.m. the opening ceremonies at the Auditorium featured a parade by Civil War veterans, a chorus of high school girls singing patriotic hymns and an address by the president of Princeton University, Woodrow Wilson. Then, throughout the day, there were events in all parts of the city—at the First Church of Englewood, at Hull House, at the Chicago Hebrew Institute, at the Hungarian Societies of Chicago and dozens of other places. African Americans met at the Seventh Regiment Armory to hear readings of Lincoln's speeches. In the evening, over ten thousand people jammed into the Dexter Park Pavilion to listen to speakers and give vent to their patriotism. With that, the Lincoln Centennial was over. Four years and one month later, Auditorium headliner Woodrow Wilson was inaugurated as president of the United States.

February 13, 1959

Bowing to a federal order, local TV stations announced they would be providing free airtime to perennial political candidate Lar Daly. Owner of a South Side chair plant, Daly had run unsuccessfully for office at least eighteen times. He first filed a complaint with the Federal Communications Commission in 1956, when he was denied equal TV time during the presidential race. Now Daly was a candidate in both the Democratic and Republican mayoral primaries. Chicago mayor Richard J. Daley had recently received time on the local CBS outlet to deliver his annual report, so the station would be giving Lar Daly thirty minutes' free time. Republican contender Timothy Sheehan was also expected to ask for time of his own. Saying that stations feared being forced to give airtime to write-in candidates, a CBS executive said that the current law was "poorly written."

February 14, 1929

This is the date of the Saint Valentine's Day Massacre. Chicago gangsters posing as cops machine-gunned seven men in a garage at 2122 North Clark Street. The dead men included six members of Bugs Moran's North Side mob and one "civilian" who liked to hang around the underworld. Moran himself was not present and put the blame on his South Side rival, Al Capone—"Only Capone kills like that," Moran said. Despite the lurid headlines, the shootings were never solved. In later years, variations on the massacre appeared in at least a dozen movies, most memorably in the comedy *Some Like It Hot*. However, Chicago mayor Richard J. Daley was not amused. During the 1960s, he arranged to have the infamous garage on Clark Street torn down, replacing it with senior citizen housing.

February 15, 1933

Chicago mayor Anton Cermak had opposed Franklin D. Roosevelt at the 1932 Democratic National Convention. Roosevelt had been nominated and elected president anyway, so now Cermak was in Miami Beach to make peace. This evening, the president-elect made a short speech from his open car to a crowd at a waterfront park. He spotted Cermak and called him over. Just then, a young anarchist named Guiseppe Zangara jumped up and fired five shots. He missed FDR but hit Cermak. The wounded mayor was bundled into the car and driven to the hospital. According to newspaper reports, he told FDR, "I'm glad it was me and not you, the country needs you." On March 6, two days after FDR's inauguration, Cermak died. Before the month was over, Zangara was dead in the electric chair. Eighty years later, there's still controversy over whether Zangara was shooting at Roosevelt or at Cermak.

February 16, 1779

Nobody knows exactly when Jean Baptiste Pointe DuSable built his cabin at the mouth of the Chicago River, so this date is as good as any. DuSable was the son of a French sailor and an enslaved African woman. After marrying a Potawatomie woman, he established a trading post in the area known as Eschecagou—which visitors mispronounced as "Chicago." His enterprise included two barns, a mill, a bakery, a workshop, a henhouse and a smokehouse. DuSable sold his holdings around 1800 and left. He died at his daughter's home in Missouri in 1818. In 2006, the Chicago City Council officially recognized DuSable as the founder of Chicago.

Jean Baptiste Pointe DuSable surveys the site of his cabin. *Photo by the author.*

February 17, 1977

Helen Vorhees Brach was a wealthy Glenview widow with no children. Her husband had made his money in the candy business. On this date, the sixty-six-year-old woman left the Mayo Clinic in Minnesota after a routine checkup. Then she disappeared. Two weeks later, the butler at her home contacted Helen's brother, and the brother filed a missing person report. After seven years, Helen was declared legally dead. Most of her $25 million estate went to her brother and various animal protection agencies. The case heated up again in 1989 during the investigation of a horse-trading scam at a suburban stable. Police found out that the stable owner had once dated Helen Brach. The man later confessed to various crimes in the horse-trading scheme and was given a thirty-year prison sentence. He denied any connection with Brach's disappearance. As of 2014, there is still no official determination of what exactly happened to Helen Brach.

February 18, 1965

A Chicago musician was in London pressing a claim for $1.12 billion. John Perring, a fifty-five-year-old drummer, told reporters he'd spent $150,000 researching the matter. The heart of the claim was £20,000 deposited with the Bank of England by his great-great-grandfather in the nineteenth century. In addition, there were proceeds from a share of East India Company profits. Perring also believed he had a right to inherit a British baronetcy, which had become extinct with the death of Sir Philip Perring in 1920. Asked whether he'd rather have the title or the money, Chicago's own Perring laughed and said, "The money."

February 19, 1894

Today, readers of the *Chicago Record* were learning how their city council worked. According to the paper, most of the seventy aldermen were open to bribes. Anyone who needed a city permit had to make a payoff. How big a bribe you paid depended on how much money your business was worth, making the bribes a type of graduated tax. The largest payoffs came from selling city franchises—legal monopolies awarded to transit companies and different utilities. A few years before, when a certain railroad franchise was up for renewal, four aldermen had collected $25,000 each. Though the system was common knowledge, aldermen demanded to be paid individually and in private so there would be no witnesses. The preferred place to carry out the transaction was the men's washroom at city hall.

Chicago has the finest aldermen that money can buy. *From* Chicago Record, *February 19, 1894.*

February 20, 1921

This evening, a mass meeting at Odd Fellows Hall discussed unemployment and corruption in the city's African American community. The recent recession had left twenty thousand blacks without jobs. R.E. Parker, editor of the *Chicago Advocate*, placed the blame on Mayor William Hale Thompson. "The mayor has simply turned his back on the black man," Parker declared. While a few blacks had gotten choice jobs because of political connections, many thousands more were starving. Parker planned on bringing a delegation to city hall to present the facts to Thompson in person. Meanwhile, the city's highest-elected black official, Alderman Louis B. Anderson, defended the mayor's record. He called Parker a "troublemaker" who was stirring up recently arrived people who didn't know any better. Anderson dismissed charges that graft flourished in the alderman's Second Ward. "If he has the proof, why doesn't he take it to the grand jury?" Anderson asked. "I'm sure [they] would be glad to get any evidence such as Parker says he has."

February 21, 1907

Michael Cassius McDonald was Chicago's gambling king and a Democratic Party kingmaker. He had been for decades. He was sixty-seven years old with a trophy wife named Dora, thirty years his junior. Dora had grown bored with her husband, taking up with a handsome young artist named Webster Guerin. At ten o'clock on this particular morning, Dora visited Webster at his studio in a Loop office building. A shot rang out. When the door to the studio was broken down, Dora was found standing over Webster's dead body. She was taken into custody and charged with murder. In true soap opera fashion, the elderly husband stood by his young wife. When Dora was finally brought to trial, it took a jury only five hours to acquit her. By then, old Mike McDonald was dead. Dora left Chicago soon after the trial and lived the rest of her life quietly.

February 22, 1965

The University of Illinois had been founded in Urbana in 1867. A Chicago branch opened at Navy Pier in 1946. The pier had limited room, and undergrads had to finish their last two years at the main campus, 130 miles away. Now in 1965, Mayor Richard J. Daley was dedicating Chicago's first full-fledged public university, the University of Illinois at Chicago Circle. About five thousand students came out to join in the day's festivities and inspect the severely modern campus buildings. Daley had been trying to get the school built since his days as a state senator. The university trustees had leaned toward a site in Garfield Park. But when Daley became mayor, he decided that a location at Harrison-Halsted would help stabilize the Loop. Despite heated protests, a good part of historic Little Italy was bulldozed, and Daley got his way. Today, the school is known simply as the University of Illinois at Chicago, since few institutions of higher learning are named after expressway interchanges.

February 23, 1905

The first Rotary Club was founded by Chicago attorney Paul P. Harris on this date. Calling together three business associates at the downtown Unity Building, Harris and the other men talked about their personal experiences. Harris then presented a plan for weekly meetings, hoping to recapture in a professional club the same type of spirit he'd enjoyed growing up in small towns. The four men decided to call themselves the Rotary Club because they planned on rotating meetings among their offices. As other members joined, a permanent meeting place was rented. Rotary soon evolved into a service organization, the first of its kind. A century after its founding, Rotary International was headquartered in Evanston and counted about 1.2 million members worldwide.

February 24, 1982

Wally Phillips was the host on WGN radio's morning drive-time show in 1975. He decided to test the powers of self-proclaimed psychics in an original way. Phillips wrote the name of a moderately famous living person on a piece of paper and locked it in a black box. On air, he challenged anyone to call in, identify the name and win a substantial cash prize. Each day, he added to the jackpot. For over six years, psychics and non-psychics took a crack at identifying the name in "Wally's Black Box." No one did. Phillips finally decided he'd made his point. On this date he revealed that the mystery name was Jean Rogers, a second-level Hollywood actress who'd starred in a couple of "Flash Gordon" serials during the 1930s. At one point during the six years, Phillips had heard Rogers was dead, so he hired a private detective to track her down. Rogers was indeed alive and later appeared on Phillips's program. The money in the black box was given to charity.

February 25, 1852

There's no evidence Mark Twain ever heard of David Kennison. Still, he may have based one of the con men in *Huckleberry Finn* on Kennison. Twain's character claimed to be the rightful king of France. Kennison's ambitions were more modest—he said that he was the last survivor of the Boston Tea Party.

David Kennison's grave marker in Lincoln Park. *Photo by the author.*

When he arrived in Chicago in 1848, the locals were thrilled to have such a celebrity among them. Kennison was given free drinks, free meals, free clothes and free rent. He repaid Chicago's generosity with stirring tales of the Revolution. Besides the Boston Tea Party, he'd been present at just about every major event in the War for Independence. Kennison died at the reported age of 115 on February 24, 1852. His military funeral the next day was the biggest Chicago had ever seen, with the entire city government and most of the forty thousand residents laying him to rest in City Cemetery. Years later, when the cemetery became Lincoln Park, it was discovered that Kennison's grave had been lost. A marker now rests at a probable location.

February 26, 1949

Over fifty thousand Chicagoans were living in unsafe firetraps. That was the message from Roy T. Christiansen, the city building commissioner. His inspectors were busy trying to eliminate fire hazards in apartment buildings. Yet the inspectors often found it impossible to locate a building owner because the owner's identity was disguised in a trust. Even when the owner was guilty of code violations, the punishment was only a fine. Christiansen said that building owners should be required to identify themselves to city inspectors. At the same time, building code violations should be made a misdemeanor, punishable by jail time. The commissioner's recommendations were endorsed by the city council and passed on to the state legislature, which had the final say in the matter.

February 27, 1979

Jane Byrne had been the city's consumer affairs commissioner until dumped by Mayor Michael Bilandic in 1977. In 1979, she challenged Bilandic in the Democratic mayoral primary. At first given no chance to beat the Machine, Byrne was helped by the weather. Two major snowstorms snarled the city. Bilandic wasn't able to get the streets cleared and was seen as an ineffective mayor. Byrne helped drive home the point by filming a TV commercial with snowflakes falling on her head. In the February 27 primary, Byrne defeated Bilandic to win the Democratic nomination. After that, the April general election was a mere formality, and Jane Byrne became Chicago's first female mayor.

February 28, 1970

As protests go, this one was orderly. Ten thousand people on the street, minor disruption, no injuries and only one arrest. Georges Pompidou, the new president of France, was in Chicago to speak at a black-tie Palmer House dinner. He'd recently agreed to sell fifty Mirage supersonic jets to Libya. Jewish groups feared that the planes would be resold to Egypt and Syria for use against Israel. Though Pompidou met with local Jewish leaders at his hotel and answered their questions, he remained firm. So as evening approached, the streets around the Palmer House were filled with demonstrators carrying signs. They seemed to be in good humor, and when Pompidou arrived, he smiled and waved at them. The dinner went on as scheduled. By the time it was over, the demonstrators had gone. Later, the French president issued a statement saying that police could have done a better job controlling the crowd. Mayor Richard J. Daley—who'd pointedly avoided meeting Pompidou—responded tersely, "Nothing occurred in Chicago for which anyone is required to apologize."

February 29, 1960

On Leap Year Day 1960, the first Playboy Club opened at 116 East Walton Street. Chicago already had one successful key club with an 1890s atmosphere, the Gaslight Club. *Playboy* magazine impresario Hugh Hefner took that theme and brought it into the Swinging Sixties. For a twenty-five-dollar fee, a member received a gold key that gave access to the Chicago club and other Playboy clubs still on the drawing board. The club offered fine food and drink, live music and standup comics. Probably the most publicized element of the club was the female servers, called Bunnies, who wore abbreviated costumes in a rabbit motif. Immediately successful, the Chicago Playboy Club drew over fifteen thousand visitors in the first month. By the end of the year, it ranked as the busiest nightclub in the world. The Playboy chain eventually grew to over thirty clubs worldwide. Changing tastes killed the Chicago club and most of the others by 1991.

March 1, 1884

On this date, the city issued a permit to construct an office building at the northeast corner of La Salle and Adams Streets. The Home Insurance Building would start a revolution. In the past, buildings had been supported by their walls. William LeBaron Jenney, architect of the new building, changed this. He built an interior metal frame as the main support of the structure, using both iron and steel. The Home Insurance Building topped off at ten floors and 138 feet in 1885. Though Jenney's building was not totally supported by the metal frame, it showed the way of the future and is commonly cited as the world's first skyscraper. In the years afterward, other architects began going higher and higher. Two additional floors were added to the Home Insurance building. In 1931, Chicago's pioneer skyscraper was torn down—to make way for a taller building.

March 2, 1953

Looking for some "action" in suburban Chicago? You didn't have to go to Cicero, Calumet City or the other traditional places. According to today's *Tribune*, there was plenty to do in the Northwest suburbs. Gambling went on all night at the Wagon Wheel on Montrose Avenue in Norwood Township. Though it looked like any other workingman's tavern from the front, the back room provided a horse-racing book, three poker tables and a roulette wheel. Other suburban betting parlors included the Ballard Inn, the Beverly Tap, the Forest Lounge and the Florentine Saloon, which boasted a singing bartender. If you tired of gambling and wanted to find a prostitute, that could be arranged. Vic's, on River Road near Higgins, was the Northwest suburbs' leading brothel. The Sunrise Inn, which posed as a tourist camp, was another well-established venue. All these businesses had one thing in common—they were located in unincorporated areas, under the jurisdiction of the Cook County sheriff. Raids weren't a problem. "If someone does set this joint up to knock it over," one bartender bragged, "everything will be as smooth as silk."

March 3, 1902

Prince Henry of Prussia, brother of the German emperor, was visiting Chicago. The city's German community planned special activities for the royal visitor, and they were dutifully reported in the press. What wasn't mentioned was the prince's most earnest request—he wanted to visit the Everleigh Club, the sumptuous Levee brothel. So after the evening's ceremonial banquet at a downtown hotel, Prince Henry and his party discretely made their way to the mansion at 2131 South Dearborn Street. In honor of their guests, the ladies of the club had prepared an entertainment celebrating the god Dionysius. When a slipper flew off a dancer's foot, one of the prince's men picked up the slipper, filled it with champagne and drank from it. The rest of the evening's activities can best be left to the imagination. However, the practice of drinking champagne out of a lady's slipper soon became a symbol of decadent sophistication.

March 4, 1837

This was the day Chicago became a city, its charter approved by the Illinois legislature. The population was 4,170. In 1833, when Chicago was organized as a town, the number of residents had been 350. The World's Fair of 1933 commemorated Chicago's founding as a town and was called the Century of Progress Exposition. However, Chicago always celebrates March 4 as its official birthday.

March 5, 1934

Where Pulaski becomes Crawford—border between Chicago and Lincolnwood. *Photo by the author.*

In December 1933, the city council voted to change Crawford Avenue to Pulaski Road. Local businessmen didn't like the costs involved in the change and got an injunction to halt the action. The Appellate Court overturned the injunction on March 5, 1934, and crews started putting up Pulaski signs. Yet the battle was hardly over. The Crawford group got a state law passed, which said property owners on a street could have the name changed if 60 percent of them signed a petition. The Crawfords then began gathering signatures. The Pulaski supporters fought back with their own legal maneuvers. In 1951, the Crawfords got the number of signatures they needed. The matter went to the Superior Court—and the judge ordered the street changed back to Crawford! The Pulaskis appealed to the Illinois Supreme Court. Finally, in November 1952, the state's highest court tossed out the petition law. Once and for all, Pulaski Road became an official Chicago street. But in some suburbs, it's still called Crawford Avenue.

March 6, 1975

Goldblatt's department store on State Street was holding its first bargain basement sale. A special purchase of 647 Bergdorf Goodman designer dresses, retailing at up to $1,900 each, was going on sale for $29.99 to $89.99. More than two hundred women were waiting. At the 9:15 a.m. opening bell, they charged the racks, grabbing armloads of dresses and heading for the changing rooms. One woman started pulling off her own dress right on the sales floor, until she realized a TV camera was pointed at her. Louis Goldblatt, one of the store owners, was watching and smiling. "I sent my people up to Filene's in Boston to study how they conduct their sales," he said. "I wanted to bring some excitement back into the retail business." He predicted that other stores would adopt the policy of buying high-end goods and selling them at bargain prices. "We'll have people all over the country talking about us," Goldblatt said.

March 7, 1911

In 1911, women could not vote in Illinois. On March 7 of that year, a group of three hundred female activists from Chicago chartered a train and traveled to Springfield to lobby the state legislature. Some were veterans of the struggle, like Grace Wilbur Trout and Margaret Dreier Robins. There was also a large contingent of young female students from the University of Chicago. The "suffrage train" made dozens of stops for impromptu speeches to the curious public. Arriving in Springfield, the women changed into evening clothes for a grand entrance at the capitol. Fifteen of them were given three minutes each to state the case for female suffrage to the all-male assembly. The lawmakers listened politely, thanked the speakers and then adjourned. The day ended with a reception at the governor's mansion. But despite the publicity given to the suffrage train, Illinois women did not gain full voting rights until 1920, when the Nineteenth Amendment to the U.S. Constitution settled the matter.

March 8, 1946

World War II was over, and inflation was being seen in food prices. Today's newspaper ad for the National Food Stores listed choice frying chickens at forty-one cents per pound and a pound of hamburger at twenty-six cents. A dozen eggs cost forty-five cents, a pound of coffee thirty-one cents. The price of a two-quart container of milk had risen to twenty-nine cents. However, most fruits and vegetables were still reasonably cheap. A ten-pound bag of potatoes sold for forty-nine cents, three bunches of carrots were seventeen cents, seven pounds of oranges were forty-nine cents. National did not yet offer S&H Green Stamps as a promotion. However, anyone who purchased six jars of strained baby food at the regular forty-seven-cent price received a free Fireking heat-proof nursing bottle—a useful premium in the time of the baby boom.

March 9, 1945

Early this morning, two men walking on the 1600 block of North Clybourn Avenue discovered Fred Walcher nailed to a cross in the shadow of the L structure. The forty-six-year-old lens grinder was alive. He was taken to the hospital, where he told police his story. It seemed that Walcher was worried about the state of civilization and had started a movement called American Industrial Democracy. He'd often said that the people needed something to wake them up, something like a crucifixion. Three men had taken him at his word and crucified him. When Walcher said he didn't blame the perpetrators, the cops became suspicious. An investigation revealed that the American Industrial Democracy movement existed mostly in Walcher's imagination. Eventually, Walcher confessed that he'd staged the crucifixion to win publicity for his cause. He was fined $100 for disorderly conduct and sank back into obscurity.

March 10, 1914

"Hog Butcher for the World/Tool Maker, Stacker of Wheat/Player with Railroads and the Nation's Freight Handler." Those are the opening lines of Carl Sandburg's poem "Chicago," first published in the March 1914 issue of *Poetry* magazine. He'd written the poem while working as a *Daily News* reporter and living in a house on Hermitage Avenue in Uptown. "Chicago" made Sandburg nationally famous. For decades afterward, local schoolteachers had their students commit it to memory.

March 11, 1930

Today, Chicago said goodbye to the Dingbat. The Dingbat was John Oberta, bootlegger, racketeer and Thirteenth Ward Republican committeeman. He'd been found shot dead in his car, along with his chauffeur, on a deserted road near Willow Springs. Now Dingbat's family and friends were giving him a royal sendoff. At his bungalow in Gage Park, Dingbat lay in a $15,000 mahogany casket with silver handles, under a blanket of orchids. Two priests of the Polish National Catholic Church conducted a brief service. The coffin was then carried out the front door and loaded into the hearse, bound for Holy Sepulchre Cemetery. Trailing behind were four carloads of flowers and a procession of autos two miles long. Police estimated that twenty thousand spectators lined the funeral route. Meanwhile, in Washington, former president William Howard Taft was being laid to rest at about the same time as Dingbat. Taft's funeral drew half as many people.

March 12, 1966

The Chicago Blackhawks defeated the New York Rangers at the Chicago Stadium today, 4–2. History was made when Hawks left wing Bobby Hull became the first National Hockey League player to score more than fifty goals in a single season. At 5:34 of the third period, Hull blasted a fifty-foot slap shot through the skates of the Ranger goalie. With that, the fans threw hats, seat cushions and other items onto the ice, and the game was delayed nearly eight minutes while workmen cleaned up the celebratory debris. Prior to Hull's record-breaking fifty-first goal, three players had shared the NHL record of fifty goals in a season—Maurice Richard, Boom Boom Geoffrion and Hull himself. Hull eventually finished the 1965–66 season with fifty-four goals.

March 13, 1921

Chicagoans were reading about the exploits of a nine-year-old chess wizard named Sammy Rzeschewski. He'd arrived in Chicago with his parents and agent, fresh from triumphs on the East Coast. Last night's simultaneous exhibition was held at the Illinois Athletic Club, which had drained its sixty-foot swimming pool and erected a platform to accommodate twenty chess tables. Sammy faced a picked group of twenty adult opponents and defeated all twenty. During his stay in Chicago, he played forty-six games and lost only one. The "boy wizard of chess" later became known as Samuel Reshevsky and was a many-time U.S. national champion.

March 14, 1926

City health commissioner Dr. Herman Bundesen was launching a project he called "human dairies." Nursing mothers who had surplus milk could sell it to the city for ten cents per ounce. The milk would then be sold to needy moms at a price based on the buyer's ability to pay. "We have gone into this project essentially for poor and orphan babies," Bundesen said. "Our purpose is not to make money, but to save lives." The program had an initial cost of $5,000, after which it would be self-sustaining.

Preparing milk for needy infants. *Author's collection.*

March 15, 1937

Blood transfusions were becoming more common in the 1930s, but blood would go stale after a while. Dr. Bernard

Fantus of Cook County Hospital knew Russia was setting up blood depots to provide patients with easier access to stored blood. In 1934, Fantus began a series of experiments to increase the storage time. Using refrigeration and various additives, he was able to preserve blood for up to ten days. By 1937, the doctor was ready to open the Blood Preservation Laboratory at County. Everything was ready—except Fantus didn't like the name! The whole thing sounded like something out of a Dracula movie. When the facility did open on March 15, it was known as the Cook County Hospital Blood Bank. The blood bank proved successful, and the concept spread worldwide.

The old Cook County Hospital. *Photo by the author.*

March 16, 1899

Joseph Medill had published the *Chicago Tribune* for forty-four years, had helped make his friend Abe Lincoln president of the United States and had even served a term as mayor of Chicago. Now Medill was dying, and he knew he was dying. As a newsman he'd always had an eye for a catchy story hook. This morning, Medill called his attending physician close to his bedside and said in a firm voice, "My last words shall be, 'What is the news?'" Medill spoke no more after that, and within ten minutes he was dead. In our time, you will find Joseph Medill's "What is the news?" referenced in nearly every collection of famous last words or book of familiar quotations. And as another well-known Chicago newsman used to say, "Now you know the *rest of the story*."

March 17, 1956

Chicago's St. Patrick's Day Parade began in 1956. Though South Siders had held a parade down 79th Street for some years, this was the first official, citywide celebration, with Mayor Richard J. Daley leading ten thousand Irish and honorary-Irish down State Street in the cold, wet, windy weather. The marchers wore hats festooned with shamrocks and swung blackthorn sticks and shillelaghs. Some of them played Irish pipes or sang Irish songs. Floats carried rugged Gaelic football players, Irish dancers and smiling Irish colleens. The parade lasted an hour. Over a quarter million spectators lined the route, while an untold number more watched on TV. The day's festivities concluded with a special Mass at Old St. Patrick's Church. Chicago St. Patrick's Day Parade was considered a grand success and continues as an annual event. And since 1961, on parade day, the city has dyed the Chicago River emerald green.

March 18, 1973

A year after its launch, Operation Whistle Stop was a success. The program of the Hyde Park–Kenwood Community Conference had distributed about eighteen thousand whistles among forty-six thousand neighborhood residents. A person threatened by a crime—or a person witnessing a crime—would blow a blast on the whistle. The sound alerted residents in the network to phone police. Within the last year, purse snatching had declined 41 percent, while theft from autos was down 37 percent. A second program called Operation Identification was also producing good results. Residents had been engraving their driver's licenses or social security numbers on valuables, then placing a sticker on the door notifying burglars that the loot here would be hard to fence. About five hundred homes had the stickers, and not one had been hit. Next on the Community Conference's agenda was a "good neighbor" plan for people on blocks to watch over one another's homes.

March 19, 1928

The most popular program of radio's golden age made its debut on Chicago station WMAQ today. *Amos 'n' Andy* was the story of two African American men who'd moved from the rural South to a large northern city. The title characters were voiced by two white men, Freeman Gosden and Charles Correll, in what they considered southern black dialect. Within a year, the show went national, and its popularity soared. Listeners really got involved in the continuing story arc. The program was so popular that many theaters would halt their movie at *Amos 'n' Andy* time and pipe the radio broadcast right into the auditorium. Gosden and Correll even made a feature film in blackface—which they afterward admitted was a mistake. As for the radio program, the reaction of African Americans was mixed, some saying they liked the show, others saying they did not. Gosden and Correll continued doing some version of the radio program until 1960. An *Amos 'n' Andy* TV show with a black cast ran for two seasons in the early 1950s but was later pulled from syndication after protests.

March 20, 1926

James Caesar Petrillo, head of the Chicago Federation of Musicians, thought his people were getting a raw deal. Many of the city's better hotels and cafés provided entertainment by professional musicians. About five years ago, some of these businesses started broadcasting the music on radio. At first, the musicians received no extra money for the broadcasts, though that was later changed and a definite fee schedule put in place. At the same time, radio stations would occasionally use amateur bands. The federation had permitted this under a "gentleman's agreement." According to Petrillo, the stations were now abusing the privilege. The fees collected by professional musicians might have to be raised. "We are willing to go more than half way to meet the demands requested in the musical line by the various station directors," Petrillo said. "At the same time, they should meet us the remainder of the way across the bridge."

March 21, 1959

Some seven thousand Cook County welfare clients were becoming familiar with a new phrase: "computer error." The Illinois Public Aid Commission had just started using one of those newfangled electronic brains, and now the blasted thing had failed to issue nearly 5 percent of the checks. The people affected were supposed to be receiving old age assistance, total disability assistance and Aid to Dependent Children payments. General assistance fund checks were not delayed because they were disbursed by a different department. Meanwhile, city and county governments were considering a plan to set up a $100,000 fund to supply emergency cash to recipients hit by the foul-up.

March 22, 1933

Today, more than two hundred Chicago public school teachers descended on the regular board of education meeting. Because the Depression had cut government tax revenue, the teachers had not been paid regularly in two years. Sometimes, they'd been given IOUs; sometimes, the board had simply skipped payday. The teachers had no legal recourse, since they were forbidden to go on strike by state law. Now the board was discussing a bill pending in the legislature, which would allow teacher strikes. The teachers were at the board meeting to show support for that bill. Things got heated. When a board member spoke out against the strike bill, the teachers stamped their feet and booed. Getting nowhere at the board meeting, the teachers next marched on city hall, where the city council was in session. After hearing the teachers state their case, the aldermen agreed to move forward on a plan to raise cash by selling tax anticipation warrants. That ended the day's protests.

March 23, 1963

Loyola University had the highest-scoring college basketball team in the country. The Ramblers were also the only major college team to have four African American starters, and that was noteworthy in 1963. In March, Loyola went into the NCAA Tournament with a 24-2 record and a No. 5 ranking. They easily beat Tennessee Tech. Their second game made news when the governor of Mississippi tried to stop his team from playing against "black" Loyola. Mississippi State played anyway, and lost. Loyola then defeated Illinois and Duke to reach the finals against Cincinnati. On March 23 at Louisville, Loyola took the court a twenty-five to one underdog. Cincinnati built up a 45–30 lead, but Loyola came back to tie the game 54–54 at the end of regulation. Play went into overtime. When forward Vic Rouse hit a basket at the buzzer, the Ramblers had won an improbable 60–58 victory. Loyola became the first Illinois school to win an NCAA Division I basketball championship. A half century later, it still is.

March 24, 1992

Ogden Avenue follows the path of an old trail. The street originally ran from Union Park southwest to the city limits and beyond. As early as the 1880s, there were plans to extend Ogden northeast to Lincoln Park. Construction on the project finally began in 1921. Hundreds of buildings were torn down and viaducts put in place at railroad crossings. A half-mile-long bridge was constructed over Goose Island and the Halsted-Division intersection. Thirteen years and millions of dollars later, the six-lane roadway was completed to its terminus at Clark and Armitage. Yet for various reasons, the Ogden extension never generated the traffic envisioned. By the 1960s, as property values in Old Town skyrocketed, the one-hundred-foot-wide swath of concrete seemed a waste of valuable real estate. In 1969, the city closed the section of Ogden north of North Avenue, and it was built over. A few years later, the street was cut back to Clybourn. Then, in 1992, chunks of concrete started falling off the Ogden bridge on Goose Island. On March 24, the city closed the bridge and later demolished it. After all the bother and all the money, only about one-third of the Ogden Avenue extension remains.

March 25, 1917

The City of Chicago had granted a franchise for operating streetcars to Chicago Surface Lines. But Chicago's parks and boulevards were governed by three independent park boards. On March 25, 1917, the new Chicago Motor Bus Company began operating the city's first commercial buses, courtesy of a franchise awarded by the Lincoln Park District. The gasoline-powered vehicles were double-decked, the top level open. Each of them had a two-man crew, a conductor to collect the ten-cent fare and a "chauffeur" to drive. Today's inaugural trip included Mayor William Hale Thompson and other dignitaries. Starting at Devon Avenue, the bus moved down Sheridan Road to Lincoln Park, through the park and over various streets until it reached its south terminal at Adams and State. After that, while the invited guests were brought back to the Edgewater Beach Hotel for a luncheon, regular revenue service began. Only eleven buses ran this first day, but the public was promised that thirty-nine more were on the way.

March 26, 1928

The spring primary season of 1928 was unusually violent, even by Chicago standards. The trouble was within the Republican ranks, where U.S. senator Charles Deneen's faction was battling Chicago mayor William Hale Thompson's group. Candidates on both sides had their homes vandalized by hand grenades. On March 21, the Deneen candidate for Nineteenth Ward committeeman was gunned down. The senator attended the March 26 funeral, then left for Washington by train. That evening, someone tossed a grenade onto the porch of Deneen's house and blasted off the front of the building. The attack of a U.S. senator's home made national headlines, bringing calls for martial law in war-torn Chicago. A week later, the Deneen slate swept the primaries. In 1928, hand grenades were nicknamed "pineapples," so ever afterward, the election was known as the Pineapple Primary.

Senator Deneen's one-time home. *Photo by the author.*

March 27, 1903

Chicago's own farm was a "white elephant." That was the opinion of City Comptroller Lawrence McGann. Years ago the city had received the Gage farm in Riverside as a gift. Yet over the past seven years, the property had operated at a $10,850 loss. Taxes on the farm were $1,800 a year. The city had never been able to collect more than $1,000 a year in rent, and the latest tenant had skipped out without paying. Today, several aldermen said they'd be willing to lease the property and work it. Comptroller McGann himself said, "There is nothing I should like better than running the Gage farm—I'd make a good farmer." Still, one Republican alderman was skeptical of the idea of government taking over a private business. "If the city can run one 200-acre farm at a loss of $1,550 a year," he asked, "at what loss would the city be able to run a $50 million transit system?"

March 28, 1929

In 1925, a new Madison Square Garden opened in New York City. Naturally, Chicago had to top it. The next year, a West Side promoter named Paddy Harmon organized a syndicate of investors to construct a giant sports arena at Madison and Wood Streets. Construction took over two years and cost $7 million. On March 28, 1929, the Chicago Stadium opened for business with a boxing card. The announced capacity was twenty-five thousand, though fire laws limited the number of people actually allowed in. As an unplanned adjunct to opening night, a burning tar barrel on the stadium's roof brought out a squad of firemen, who extinguished the blaze without bothering the people inside. The Chicago Stadium became a popular venue for sporting events, concerts, political conventions and other large gatherings. It was torn down in 1994, replaced by the United Center across the street.

March 29, 1987

Today, Chicago got some good news and some bad news. The good news was that Chicago had the nation's wealthiest suburb. The bad news was that Chicago also had the nation's poorest suburb. These facts were detailed in urbanologist Pierre deVise's latest study, *The Geography of Wealth and Poverty in Suburban America, 1979 to 1985.* DeVise examined the country's fifteen largest metropolitan areas. Kenilworth had the highest per capita income of any suburb, $44,520, while south suburban Ford Heights ranked dead last at $4,523 per capita. The study ranked Glencoe as number twenty nationally on the wealthy suburb list, with Winnetka at number twenty-two. Few people were surprise that the North Shore was doing well. What shocked Chicagoans was how much suburban poverty was at their doorstep. Robbins and Phoenix, two other south suburbs, were also near the bottom of the income list. As always, deVise's statistical methods drew some criticism, since he ranked the suburbs solely on per capita income. "We have 261 towns in northeastern Illinois," one critic noted, "and no two are alike."

March 30, 2003

Meigs Field was Chicago's downtown airport, located on a man-made peninsula that had been used for the 1933–34 World's Fair. Opened in 1948, Meigs became the country's busiest single-runway facility, mostly serving private planes. Then, in 1994, Mayor Richard M. Daley proposed closing Meigs and returning the site to its original purpose as a park. Daley's plan set off a heated battle between aviation interests and environmental groups. Lawsuits were filed, compromise solutions proposed and discarded. Nine years passed, and the mayor decided he'd waited long enough. In the small hours of March 30, 2003, city bulldozers rolled onto Meigs and carved huge X marks onto the runway. Now planes could not land or take off—enough talk! One inbound flight was forced to divert, and sixteen parked planes had to depart using the taxiway. The FAA fined the city $33,000 for closing Meigs without sufficient notice. The mayor was called arrogant and highhanded for shutting down the airfield in such a peremptory manner. But Meigs Field was gone and has not returned.

March 31, 1981

The violence was continuing at the Cabrini-Green housing project, with eleven people killed and thirty-seven injured so far this year. So this evening, Mayor Jane Byrne and her husband moved into a fourth-floor apartment in one of the high-rises. They moved without fanfare, except for the squadron of police and security guards clearing the way. Later, the cops broke up a planned fight between two rival gangs in the mayor's building. Byrne lived in the project for three weeks before moving back to her own residence. Though political rivals dismissed the mayor's sojourn as political grandstanding, it did bring some tranquility to the projects.

April 1, 1911

Because of Chicago's rapid growth, by 1900 the city's address numbers were a mess. There was no single system in use. Different parts of the city numbered street addresses from the lakeshore, from the Chicago River or from a major street, like Western Avenue. Edward P. Brennan came up with a unified system, in which State Street was one baseline, Madison Street was the other and all address numbers were based on the distance from one of the baselines. In 1909, the Brennan system was adopted in all Chicago, except for the Loop. Downtown businesses were given extra time to implement the change because of the expense involved. The revised Loop addresses became effective on April 1, 1911. Chicago now had the simplest, most efficient street numbering system of any great city in the world.

April 2, 1948

College GI Joe was a gentleman and a scholar. That was local reaction to remarks made by a Miami University official at a Stevens Hotel conference. The official claimed students who were military veterans had brought to campus problems of drunkenness, gambling, disorderly conduct and commando innovations. Though nobody seemed to know what "commando innovations" meant, spokesmen at the University of Chicago, Northwestern, Illinois and other schools said the vets actually got better marks and were more mature. As for drunkenness, a Roosevelt dean said he was "astonished that the problem is as slight as it is." Over at DePaul, three hundred students signed a letter reminding critics that these men had fought to defend freedom. The veterans themselves seemed amused by the controversy. "None of us have time to do all that," laughed Richard Sandquist, marine vet and Illinois student. "We're too busy studying and working after school hours to be anything but adult about getting an education."

April 3, 1939

After nearly a decade of uncertainty, Chicago's banks were recovering. The Federal Reserve Bank of Chicago counted $1.5 billion in deposits, which made it the ninth-largest financial institution in the English-speaking world. Continental Illinois National Bank and Trust was the next highest local bank on the list at number twelve, followed by the First National Bank of Chicago (number fourteen), Northern Trust Company (number forty) and Harris Trust & Savings Bank (number forty-nine). If Europe would only stay peaceful, the future looked bright.

April 4, 1912

Three people were killed and twenty others injured today at a railroad crossing accident on Kedzie Avenue near 37th Street. The city had ordered the Chicago & Alton Railroad to build viaducts where its tracks crossed major streets. The railroad had delayed, citing poor weather and other excuses. The latest accident occurred when a northbound Kedzie streetcar stopped at the C&A crossing for a passing freight. Following standard procedure, the conductor got off the car to signal the motorman when the track was clear. The conductor waived the car through after the freight passed, but he hadn't noticed another freight approaching on a parallel track. The second freight slammed into the car, toppling it over and crushing it. The sound of the crash brought people from nearby buildings running to the scene, and the injured were transported to nearby hospitals in carriages. The three people killed turned out to be members of a single family. The C&A tracks at Kedzie and 37th were eventually elevated, as were most of Chicago's other railroad crossings.

April 5, 1955

The first Mayor Daley—Richard J. *Author's collection.*

Chicagoans didn't know very much about the man they elected their forty-eighth mayor on April 2, 1955. Richard J. Daley had grown up in Bridgeport, served in the state legislature and as county clerk and steadily climbed through the Democratic Party, becoming county chairman in 1953. He'd ousted incumbent mayor Martin Kennelly in the primary and now had beaten charismatic alderman Robert Merriam in the general election. There were predictions that Daley would bring back the bad old days of corrupt city government. Other seers said the new mayor was smart enough to get the city moving again while attending to the necessities of politics. All that lay in the future. Daley was known to be totally unsentimental where politics was concerned, but he did keep one souvenir from this first mayoral election. For the rest of his life, his car carried license plate "708 222"— the number of votes he polled today.

April 6, 1926

Big Bill Thompson always knew how to put on a show. The former mayor planned on running for his old office in 1927. His one-time pal Fred Lundin was grooming Dr. John Dill Robertson for the post. Today's rally at the Cort Theatre was supposed to be about the 1926 U.S. Senate primary. But the audience knew something else was up when Thompson walked on stage carrying two caged rats. He pointed at one rat, calling him Doc and saying the rat hadn't had a bath in twenty years. The audience roared, and Big Bill addressed the other rat. "Don't hang your head, Fred," he said. "Wasn't I the best friend you ever had?" Thompson went on with his stand-up routine for twenty minutes, the crowed urging him on to greater insults. He closed by saying that he'd wanted to bring six rats—"but Fred and Doc ate the other four." That brought down the house. The next day Big Bill's Rat Show was reported across the country.

April 7, 1954

Henry Ford II was in the city today to inspect his company's aircraft engine plant on the Southwest Side. Joined by air force brass and other company execs, as well as sixty reporters, Ford's tour of the eighty-seven-acre plant lasted two hours. Tests were being completed on the latest model jet engine, with production to begin shortly. A Ford spokesman said that the engine project would be carried through into 1957. At present, the plant employed sixteen thousand workers. Though there might be some layoffs this fall, when the first phase of production was completed, it was still too early to say how many jobs might be lost. At a news conference after the tour, Ford was asked for his views on the current recession. "I don't think there's any recession," he replied.

April 8, 1964

Today, the Chicago Board of Education voted unanimously to approve "in general principle" a special report on school integration. A committee headed by University of Chicago sociologist Philip M. Hauser had come up with thirteen recommendations. The most controversial proposal was that the city modify its long-standing tradition of neighborhood schools. The board gave school superintendent Benjamin Willis responsibility for implementing the Hauser Report.

April 9, 1941

In 1941, local communities decided whether they wanted to observe daylight saving time. Chicago pushed its clocks ahead one hour on the last Sunday in April and turned them back on the last Sunday in September. Now, many Chicagoans wanted to extend DST a month, to the last Sunday in October. Most people questioned favored the change, citing many positive results. There would be fewer traffic accidents. There would be less crime. The economy would be helped, with people staying out later and spending more money. In the Loop, bank and department store employees would have an extra hour of softball time in Grant Park. High school football teams could practice under natural sunlight instead of artificial lights. Golfers, tennis players and soccer players were interviewed, and all came out in favor of more DST. In May, the Chicago City Council voted to extend local DST the extra month. A national DST law was finally adopted in 1967.

April 10, 1865

The news reached Chicago on Sunday evening. General Lee had surrendered and the Civil War was over! The city celebrated with impromptu parades, gunshots, bonfires and straw-filled dummies (with the names of Rebel leaders) hung from trees. At midnight, the hundred guns of the Dearborn Light Artillery boomed and continued through the night. Hardly any of the city's 200,000 residents got any sleep. On Monday, people felt like taking a holiday, so most businesses closed. Government buildings were decorated with bunting, and street vendors selling tiny American flags couldn't keep up with the demand. Another night of celebration followed. Tuesday came, and the city began returning to normal.

April 11, 1935

The *Garfieldian*, a West Side community newspaper, was offering a special excursion to the Shrine of the Little Flower in Royal Oak, Michigan. The $14.90 price included roundtrip rail fare, all meals, one night at the Leland Hotel in Detroit and a side trip to Canada. The highlight was a Palm Sunday Mass at the shrine, home of "radio priest" Father Charles Coughlin. The excursion was scheduled to depart Chicago on the Grand Trunk at 2:00 p.m. Saturday, returning at 9:30 p.m. the next evening.

April 12, 1924

A Chicagoan might become the next president of the United States. One year into his term as the city's mayor, William E. Dever had already become a national figure. A report out of Washington today said that Dever's successful war on bootleggers had put him on the short list of contenders for the 1924 Democratic nomination. Dever was being hailed as "the mayor who cleaned up Chicago."

Mayor William E. Dever. *Author's collection.*

April 13, 1992

By 1991, the freight tunnels beneath the Loop were abandoned and mostly forgotten. That December, a contractor sinking wooden pilings into the river near Kinzie Street cracked one of the tunnel walls. The city was notified, but the crack seemed to be minor, so nothing was done about fixing it. Four months later—April 13, 1992, at 6:00 a.m.—the Chicago River burst through the Kinzie Street crack and began pouring through the tunnel network. At street level, everything looked normal. Below ground, the surging water knocked out gas and electric lines and flooded basements. Trading was suspended at the exchange, government offices shut down, businesses closed and sent their employees home—but not on the subway, since the power there was knocked out. At 11:00 a.m., the river locks were opened, allowing the Chicago River to resume its natural course and gradually stabilize the water level in the tunnels. Pumping them out took weeks. The price tag for damaged goods, repairs and lost business exceeded $100 million.

April 14, 1909

Professional wrestling was a recognized, competitive sport in 1909. Tonight, more than twenty thousand fans squeezed into the Dexter Park Pavilion to watch Frank Gotch defend his heavyweight championship. His opponent was Yussif Manhout, better known as the Terrible Turk. The match was the best of three falls. Though 1909 wrestling matches were hard-fought and scientific, they weren't often flashy. In the first round, the two men rushed each other, broke a few holds and bounced off the ropes, until Gotch pinned the Turk at the eight-minute mark. After a ten-minute break, they went at it again. The champ was now using the half nelson and the crotch grip. This time it took Gotch nine minutes and ten seconds to again pin the Turk. When the bell rang to signal Gotch's victory, several men rushed into the ring and carried the triumphant hero to his dressing room. The Dexter Park Pavilion rocked with prolonged cheers. In 1909, wrestling really was wrestling.

April 15, 1955

The McDonald Brothers had started a small chain of California fast-food restaurants in the 1940s. Ray Kroc, a Chicago sales executive, convinced them to franchise the operation and go national. The first of these "new" McDonald's opened in Des Plaines on April 15, 1955. The rest of the company's history is well known. Though the original Des Plaines McDonald's was later torn down, there's a replica museum near the original site.

Replica museum near the site of the first McDonald's in Des Plaines. *Photo by the author.*

April 16, 1958

The Calumet Skyway was dedicated on this date. Building the seven-and-a-half-mile elevated highway had taken two years and cost $101 million. The morning's ceremonies began at 10:45 a.m. at the Indiana end. With four hundred invited guests present, Mayor Richard J. Daley and the Indiana lieutenant governor cut the ribbon, the toll barriers were raised and the skyway was open to traffic. The first vehicle through was a school bus carrying thirty-one fifth graders and two teachers from the Neil Elementary School, who'd written the mayor to ask for the honor. The official motorcade then followed. Actually, the City of Chicago did not have the legal authority to build a toll highway. However, the city did have the right to operate toll bridges. So technically, the Southeast Side's highway in the sky was a toll bridge over the Calumet River—with very long approach ramps.

Chicago Skyway toll bridge.
Author's collection.

April 17, 1921

Thirty thousand people braved crisp winds to march down Michigan Avenue in support of Irish independence from Great Britain today. The parade was sponsored by the American Association for the Recognition of the Irish Republic, whose first convention was opening at the Medinah Temple. A number of heroes from the struggle had come over from Ireland to participate, and they were joined by uniformed World War I veterans, a detachment of mounted police, young women in traditional costumes and a number of elaborate floats. The marchers carried signs highlighting Irish contributions to America's own struggles, such as, "Thirty-six per cent of Washington's army was Irish," or "One-fourth of the officers in General Jackson's army in the War of 1812 were Irish." Other banners were frankly critical of Great Britain: "Burn everything British but their coal." As the parade moved down from the Water Tower to 14th Street, many spectators stepped off the curb to join in the line. The organizers pronounced the parade a grand success in publicizing their cause.

April 18, 1924

At 7:30 p.m. on this Friday evening, fireman Francis Leavy was washing a window at Engine Company No. 107 when the alarm rang. The fire was at Curran Hall on Blue Island Avenue, and the firemen rushed off to fight it. During the blaze, a wall collapsed, killing eight of the men. Leavy was one of them. The day after the fire, back at the firehouse, one of the men noticed a handprint on the window Leavy had left half-washed. The man tried scrubbing it out, but the print stayed. From then on, so the legend went, every fireman assigned to the firehouse tried to remove the ghostly handprint but couldn't do it. It's said that Leavy's thumbprint was obtained from his personnel records, and the print on the window was a perfect match. Finally, in 1944, a newsboy threw a paper through the window and shattered it. Though the date is uncertain, there are those who'll tell you that this happened on April 18, 1944—twenty years to the day after Francis Leavy's death.

April 19, 1963

Carl Sandburg Village was built as a buffer. Urban blight was encroaching on the Gold Coast, so sixteen acres bounded by Clark, Division, La Salle and North were cleared. Nine high-rises with a total of 2,600 units went up on the site, at a cost of $40 million. The first ten families moved into the first building on April 19, 1963. And the gamble worked! Instead of blight spreading east to the Gold Coast, gentrification spread west from Carl Sandburg Village.

April 20, 1932

As the Great Depression moved into its third year, unemployed Chicagoans were finding new ways to make ends meet. Some of them were becoming farmers. The Cook County Board was setting aside sections of its forest preserve to be plowed, with local relief agencies distributing seed to any needy person willing to work the land. International Harvester had leased property on the Southwest Side, so that some of its 4,500 laid-off employees might have a section to cultivate. Meanwhile, out in the neighborhoods, community leaders were becoming active in the back-to-the-soil movement. So were organizations like the Red Cross, the Urban League and the Cook County Federation of Women's Clubs. City people were planting gardens in backyards and vacant lots. Potatoes, turnips, carrots and parsnips were the most popular crops. Instead of waiting passively around for a handout, Chicagoans were taking the initiative in working their way out of the hard times.

April 21, 1855

In 1855, Levi Boone was elected Chicago's mayor on the anti-immigrant American Party ticket. Once in office, he went to work restoring his version of American values. He fired all foreign-born policemen and raised the saloon license fee by 600 percent. Next, he started enforcing the law that banned public drinking on Sundays. Saloonkeepers who refused to close were arrested. Most of them were German. When their cases came to trial on April 21, hundreds of other Germans began marching from the North Side toward the downtown courthouse. The police drove them back over the river, and the mayor ordered the bridges raised, trapping the Germans on the North Side. The Germans regrouped; the police regrouped. Then, the bridges were lowered, the Germans stormed across and the fight was on. Shots were fired, and skulls were bashed. The battle lasted an hour, until the police once again drove the protesters north of the river. The so-called Lager Beer Riot ended in a victory for Mayor Boone. But in the next city election, the mayor and his party were voted out of office.

April 22, 1948

A series of *Sun-Times* articles had been exposing the dangerous condition of the city's used cars. Today, the Greater Chicago Used Car Dealers Association launched a new inspection program on all vehicles resold to the public. Brakes, lights, horns, wipers, tires and other equipment were being checked. A car meeting standards would get a safety sticker on its windshield, then be driven to the official city facility for another inspection and a city safety sticker. "The city testing lanes have special equipment for certain tests we couldn't make," the association president said. "Ours will take other factors into consideration, [such as] faults in glass and in frames, which quicker city inspection might miss." The program was being adopted because quick-buck used car dealers were damaging the reputation of honest dealers.

City auto inspector checking headlights. *Author's collection.*

April 23, 1893

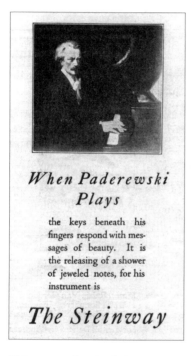

When Paderewski Plays

the keys beneath his fingers respond with messages of beauty. It is the releasing of a shower of jeweled notes, for his instrument is

The Steinway

Thirty years after the Columbian Exposition, Paderewski still plays Steinway. *Author's collection.*

The whole argument was so silly. Ignacy Jan Paderewski, the world's most famous pianist, had agreed to perform at the Columbian Exposition, without a fee. He was under contract with Steinway and assumed he'd use one of its pianos. But on April 23, with the concert a week away, the bureaucrats running the fair demanded Paderewski play on one of the "official exhibitor" pianos or not at all. Paderewski somehow kept his temper at the insult and said he was still willing to perform, but it would have to be on a Steinway. Though one newspaper thought the pianist was being a spoiled prima donna, most Chicagoans felt that fair officials were looking a gift horse in the mouth. The bureaucrats finally gave in. Paderewski performed at the fair on his Steinway—brilliantly, as usual.

April 24, 1989

Richard M. Daley was the eldest son of five-term Chicago mayor Richard J. Daley. The younger Daley was elected a state senator in 1972 and then Cook County state's attorney in 1981. He made his first try for his father's old office in 1983 but lost in the Democratic primary to Harold Washington. By 1989, with Washington dead, State's Attorney Daley ran for mayor again. Building a coalition of party regulars, lakefront independents and Latinos, Daley pledged to bring the city together after the political divisiveness of the last decade. This time, he won the Democratic primary. In the three-candidate general election, Daley polled an impressive 55 percent of the vote. On this date—his forty-seventh birthday—Richard M. Daley was sworn in as Chicago's fifty-fourth mayor.

April 25, 2008

While Alaskans talked about their Bridge to Nowhere, Chicago already had its own version over the West Side Metra tracks near Paulina. The isolated structure, connected to nothing on either side, looked like something from a giant's erector set. Actually, the bridge was a remnant of the 1895 Metropolitan L line to Logan Square. Service here was abandoned when the Milwaukee Avenue subway opened in 1951. But though the rest of the elevated structure was torn down, it was simpler and cheaper to leave the bridge in place. So now Chicago's own Bridge to Nowhere had sat unused for over fifty-seven years—longer than it was used by trains.

Chicago's "Bridge to Nowhere." *Photo by the author.*

April 26, 1951

On this day, over three million people lined Chicago's streets to welcome General Douglas MacArthur. President Truman had relieved MacArthur from his command in the Korea War when the general's policy criticisms became public. MacArthur had gone to Washington to report to Congress. Now, he was touring the country. The general's plane touched down at Midway at noon, and then he was off on a motorcade to his downtown hotel. A long, meandering route was chosen so that the maximum number of people might witness his passage. That evening, MacArthur spoke to an enthusiastic gathering at Soldier Field. He restated his call for a decisive victory in Korea. Applause interrupted him nineteen times. When he was finished, a fireworks display brought the event to a close. The next day, MacArthur was gone. And over sixty years later, his triumphant visit remains the biggest celebration for a single person Chicago has ever seen.

April 27, 1977

In 1977, the National Socialist Party of America was a tiny neo-Nazi group of perhaps one hundred people. When the City of Chicago banned party members from speaking in Marquette Park, the Nazis announced they would rally in Skokie on May 1. Since a majority of the suburb's residents were Jewish—and many were Holocaust survivors—village officials went to court on April 27 to stop the rally. The village also passed a series of ordinances designed to limit hate groups. The Nazis responded with their own lawsuits, saying their free-speech rights were being violated. The American Civil Liberties Union supported the Nazi suit on principle, even though many of its own members were Jewish. The various legal maneuvers took more than a year. In 1978, the U.S. Court of Appeals ordered Skokie to allow the Nazi demonstration. Instead, the Nazis accepted a permit for a march through downtown Chicago, which lasted all of ten minutes.

April 28, 1936

Over two hundred greens keepers and laborers walked off the job at nine North Shore golf courses in a strike for higher pay. The action was being coordinated by Local 152 of the Hod-carriers and Building and Common Laborers' Union, which was attempting to organize the men. The workers were currently earning forty-seven cents per hour for a nine-hour day. They demanded seventy-five cents per hour for an eight-hour day, with time-and-a-half on Saturday and double-time on Sunday. Thomas R. Wylie of Exmoor, spokesman for the nine clubs, said they were willing to pay fifty-five cents per hour and meet the other demands, though they would not recognize the union. "The attempt to organize our golf course employees is a racket," Wylie declared. "If we give in, this will only be the beginning—they'll organize the caddies next." Forty members of Exmoor said they were ready to cut the grass themselves in the event the workers stayed out. Police in Lake Forest and Highland Park were already guarding the golf courses in case of any disturbances. A union spokesman denied there'd been any threats made and insisted that the strike would be conducted peacefully.

April 29, 1907

Police Chief George Shippy announced that his men would be censoring questionable entertainment. Vaudeville houses were presenting lewd sketches. The five-cent theaters were running "blood and thunder" movies depicting holdups and other violent acts. Undercover police would attend shows and report back to the chief. Proprietors who did not clean up the performances would have their licenses revoked. Such vile entertainment had "a great effect on the boys and girls," Shippy explained. As part of his battle for decency, the chief also told reporters that two opium parlors on the West Side had been closed down.

April 30, 1926

Bessie Coleman came to Chicago from Texas in 1915, part of the great migration of African Americans to the cities of the North. She wanted to be a pilot. When no American flying school would accept her, Coleman went to France. She returned to the United States with her pilot's license in 1921, embarking on a career as a stunt flier. Young, attractive and extroverted, she became a headline attraction on the barnstorming circuit. Coleman was in Florida for an air show on April 30, 1926. Before the show she went up in her plane to scout the area. A few minutes into the flight, the plane went into a spin, Coleman was thrown from the open cockpit and fell to her death. Her body was returned to Chicago, where more than ten thousand mourners filed past her coffin. In 2014, one of the streets at O'Hare Airport is named Bessie Coleman Drive.

May 1, 1918

When the United States entered World War I in 1917, anti-German feeling swept the country. One example was name changing—German measles became European measles, sauerkraut became liberty cabbage, the dachshund was changed to the liberty pup. In Chicago, Bismarck Elementary School had been standing on the corner of Central Park and Armitage for twenty years. Once war was declared, however, the long-dead Otto von Bismarck was seen as an example of German militarism who didn't deserve to be commemorated in an American school. Someone suggested the name be changed to honor General Frederick Funston, a hero of the Philippine conflict and the San Francisco earthquake, who had just died. A few members of the school board thought the name change was silly and delayed action. The full board overrode the objections, and Bismarck School officially became Funston School on May 1, 1918.

"Carved in stone?" Where Funston replaced Bismarck. *Photo by the author.*

May 2, 1921

Today, the Field Museum opened its magnificent new home in Grant Park. Originally housed in a Jackson Park building left over from the 1893 Columbian Exposition, the museum began as a glorified attic preserving remnants of the fair. After merchant prince Marshall Field became a major benefactor, the collection grew to embrace all aspects of natural history. In 1917, the trustees decided to relocate to a more central site in Grant Park. Now, everything was ready. The first day was reserved for eight thousand invited guests, and all afternoon, cabs and private cars bounced over the unpaved park roads to inspect the city's latest landmark and the wonders within—"mounted birds and prehistoric animals, skeletons, Egyptian coffins and mummies," according to one reporter. The opening-day visitors were visibly impressed. The next day, Chicago's Field Museum was thrown open to the world.

May 3, 1973

The Sears Tower (left) joins Chicago's skyline. *Photo by the author.*

In the late 1960s, Sears wanted its headquarters out of Lawndale. The company looked at several suburban sites and then decided to relocate to Wacker Drive, just west of the Loop. The original plan was to construct two separate buildings. But Sears had always taken pride in its identity as a retailing giant—when the company started a radio station, the call letters were WLS, for World's Largest Store. The two-building idea was scrapped in favor of a single 1,454-foot tower, the tallest building in the world. Construction began in 1970 and lasted three years. Today's topping-off ceremony featured a final girder containing the signatures of thirteen thousand people who'd taken part in the project. As the girder was lifted into place, a chorus of electrical workers called the Tower Bums sang a song they composed titled "The Tallest Rock." The Sears Tower remained world's tallest building until passed by an Asian structure in 1996.

May 4, 1886

Two striking workers were killed in a confrontation with police at the McCormick Reaper Works on May 3, 1886. A local anarchist group called a protest meeting, and the next evening two thousand people gathered in Haymarket Square on Randolph Street. The rally lasted three hours, and about three hundred stragglers were left when the final speaker began his remarks. Now, a contingent of police arrived. When the officer in charge ordered the crowd to disperse, someone threw a bomb. The bomb exploded; the police started shooting. Five minutes later, eight cops were dead and sixty wounded. The number of civilians killed or wounded was never determined. And neither was the identity of the bomb thrower or whether the police had recklessly hit some of their own people. Eight anarchists were later charged with murder for their part in the "Haymarket Riot," tried and convicted. Four of them were hanged and another committed suicide. The remaining three were imprisoned until pardoned by Governor John P. Altgeld in 1893.

Haymarket Square. *Author's collection.*

May 5, 1905

On this date, a young lawyer named Robert S. Abbott began publishing a weekly newspaper for Chicago's thirty thousand African Americans. He called it the *Chicago Defender*, and it was literally a one-man operation. Abbott wrote the copy, set the type, folded the papers and sold them himself. The first issues were four pages long, devoted mainly to news about local people within the black community. The *Defender* was originally sold by subscription. Within a few years, Abbott had 1,000 subscribers and moved into newsstand sales. He also began printing more stories about social issues. African Americans were starting to move from the rural South to the industrial North, and the paper encouraged the migration. Abbott's stories were so persuasive that the southern ruling class tried to suppress the paper. By the 1920s, the *Defender* had become a daily in Chicago and also published a weekly national edition. Circulation was over 200,000.

May 6, 1985

The state wanted to centralize all its Chicago offices in one place, so Helmut Jahn was hired to design the new headquarters. Jahn's State of Illinois Building opened across Randolph from city hall on this date. Critics either loved or hated the bold postmodern architecture, though everyone was awed by the soaring atrium inside. In 1993, the building was renamed the James R. Thompson Center, after the longtime governor.

May 7, 1896

Herman Mudgett was better known by his alias, Dr. Henry H. Holmes. During the 1893 Columbian Exposition, he opened a hotel at 63rd and Wallace, with the announced purpose of providing lodging for visitors to the fair. What he really had in mind was something more sinister. Lodgers at Holmes's hotel had a way of disappearing, particularly if they were women. Holmes left the city after the fair, putting a custodian in charge of his building. In November 1894, he was arrested in connection with a Philadelphia murder. Back in Chicago, police began an investigation of the 63rd Street hotel. They found evidence that Holmes was a serial killer, who had systematically tortured and killed an unknown number of people. The press dubbed the building the "Murder Castle." Estimates of the number of victims ranged from twenty up to two hundred. Holmes was put on trial in the Philadelphia murder case, found guilty and hanged on May 7, 1896. His Murder Castle was torn down in the 1930s, replaced by a post office.

May 8, 1934

Though Samuel Insull had started out as Thomas Edison's personal secretary, his talent was financial, not scientific. Insull helped build America's electrical industry, and by the 1920s, he controlled a vast utilities empire based in Chicago. Then the stock market crashed. Thousands of small investors in Insull's companies were wiped out, and someone had to take the blame. Late in 1932, while Insull was in London, a Cook County grand jury indicted him for fraud and embezzlement. Rather than wait to be extradited, he skipped out of England and dodged authorities for over a year. He was finally nabbed in Turkey. On May 8, 1934, Insull arrived back in Chicago to face the music. He claimed he'd done nothing wrong. He had lost money like everyone else and was now being made a scapegoat by demagogue politicians. That didn't matter. Insull was tried three separate times, in three different courts. He was acquitted all three times. He died of a heart attack in a Paris subway station in 1938, with eighty-four cents in his pocket.

May 9, 1909

The *Chicago Tribune* published a short interview with a lady named Sarah Warrell on May 4, 1909. Warrell talked about the new holiday being celebrated in Philadelphia and San Francisco, Mother's Day. The holiday was being observed this coming May 9 —the second Sunday in May—to honor all mothers. Warrell asked Chicagoans to wear white carnations this Sunday. Since time was short, she urged ministers, teachers and charitable institutions to get the word out. Five days later, when May 9 arrived, thousands of people throughout the city sported the white carnation. Some groups, like the YMCA and the Grand Army of the Republic, had enlisted their entire memberships. Pastors mentioned Mother's Day in sermons, and in Oak Park, the First Presbyterian Church was filled with the symbolic flower. Carnations were also distributed at various hospitals and orphanages. With less than a week's publicity, the first Chicago Mother's Day was a great success. The following year, Governor Deneen declared the day a state holiday. Not to be outdone by a Republican, Chicago mayor Carter Harrison Jr. issued his own Mother's Day proclamation the year after that.

May 10, 1947

When Harry met Sally? How about when Nelson met Simone? In 1947, Chicagoan Nelson Algren was an acclaimed author of realistic fiction. Simone de Beauvoir was a French feminist writer traveling in America. One of Simone's friends suggested she get in touch with Algren in Chicago. After a few comic misunderstandings, they became lovers—on May 10, 1947, the date they would always call their anniversary. Since neither of them wanted to relocate, for many years they carried on a transatlantic love affair. Nelson died in 1981, Simone five years later. She was buried wearing the ring Nelson had given her.

May 11, 1920

Big Jim Colosimo was just another hustler hanging out on the 22nd Street Levee. His break came in 1902 when he married the city's leading madam. Big Jim expanded his wife's operation and went into the gambling business. Later, he opened a café at 2126 South Wabash Avenue that became a chic dining spot for the city's elite to sample the latest exotic craze: Italian food. Big Jim also became a political power in the First Ward. Flush with success, in the spring of 1920, he dumped his wife and married a young singer. A few weeks later, on the afternoon of May 11, he went to the café to await a delivery. One of the employees heard a shot, followed the sound and found Big Jim dead. The police immediately suspected the first Mrs. Colosimo but soon turned their attention to Johnny Torrio, Big Jim's trusted lieutenant. Nothing could be proven, so Torrio wound up taking over Big Jim's empire. The man thought to have actually pulled the trigger was a young friend of Torrio named Al Capone.

May 12, 1930

The Adler Planetarium was opened to the public on this date. The facility was a gift to the city from Max Adler, a Sears vice-president who'd been impressed by the new night-sky projector he'd seen operating in Europe. Chicago's planetarium was the first to be built in the Western Hemisphere and was a big hit during the Century of Progress Exposition a few years later.

Adler Planetarium. *Author's collection.*

May 13, 1917

The United States had entered World War I. Now, Chicago's sons were heeding President Wilson's call to "make the world safe for democracy." At Fort Sheridan in the northern suburbs, over 2,000 men were beginning officers' training, under the watchful eyes of regular army personnel. At the end of three months, the new officers would be placed in charge of various units, such as engineers, artillery, infantry or cavalry. Back in the city, army enlistments were heavy. At one recruiting station on the Northwest side, the line of volunteers stretched a full block down Milwaukee Avenue, with 187 men taking the oath in a single day. Many of the new recruits were young Poles. Besides fighting the enemies of the United States, many of them saw a chance to help Poland regain its independence. The country had gotten by with a peacetime military force of 200,000. By the time the fighting ended in November 1918, over 4.3 million Americans would be under arms.

May 14, 1920

Mayor William Hale Thompson celebrated his fifty-first birthday today by dedicating the new Michigan Avenue Bridge. The bridge was the latest part of Burnham's Plan of Chicago to become reality. It was actually two parallel bridges that operated independently, 220 feet long and double-decked. The design was based on the monumental Pont Alexandre III in Paris. Ceremonies began at 4:00 p.m., when the mayor and other officials got into cars at Congress Plaza and began a motorcade up the avenue. They stopped at the bridge so Thompson could cut the red, white and blue ribbon hanging across the roadway. That was the signal for airplanes to fly over and "bomb" the bridge with confetti. A calliope pumped out rousing tunes, and people cheered. Then the mayor's party drove across the span, followed by four thousand cars representing interested organizations and everyday citizens. Evening fireworks brought the big day to a close.

May 15, 1899

The newly opened golf links at Jackson Park were proving popular. The nine-hole layout was the first public course west of the Alleghenies. Students from the nearby University

of Chicago were organizing their own golfing club. So were the professors. Many women were playing, with their husbands or with their lady friends. Gratified by the turnout, the South Park Commissioners were considering expanding the course to a full eighteen holes. For now, the golf at Jackson Park would continue to be free.

Jackson Park Golf Links.
Author's collection.

May 16, 1983

Harold Washington had just taken office as the city's first African American mayor. He was also a reform Democrat who'd beaten the party regulars. For years, the city council had been a rubber stamp for whoever was mayor. But when Washington tried to purge three council kingpins from their leadership positions, one of the three men fought back. Ed Vrdolyak assembled a coalition of twenty-nine aldermen—all party regulars and all white—and took control of the council. The Vrdolyak Twenty-nine then shut out the mayor's allies from all important committee chairs. Judge James Murray of the Circuit Court was called in to straighten matters out. On May 16, the judge ruled that the council could make committee assignments in any matter it wished but that the mayor could then veto funding for the council. The judge said that any differences between the two sides should be worked out around the bargaining table. The Vrdolyak Twenty-nine seemed pleased by the ruling, while the mayor himself had no immediate comment. Thus ended the first skirmish in a contentious four years that would be labeled Council Wars.

May 17, 1954

Today, the Chicago Housing Authority announced plans for a project called Stateway Gardens. The new public housing would cover eight blocks in the Bronzeville neighborhood, bounded by 35th, State, Pershing and the Rock Island Railroad embankment. Until now, most of Chicago's public housing had been low-rise, no more than one or two floors. Stateway Gardens was different. The planners wanted to have plenty of open space, to give the feel of "a suburb in the city." The buildings here would be high-rise—eight towers of sixteen floors each, for a total of 1,649 apartments. The CHA was also talking about clearing the entire State Street corridor all the way south to 63rd Street, though nothing was definite yet. If more public housing projects were to be built there, the units would likely follow the Stateway model. High-rise housing on landscaped plazas was the fashionable trend in urban design.

May 18, 1860

Chicago was playing host to its first national political convention. The Republicans were gathering at the Wigwam, a newly built wooden barn on Lake Street. Senator William Seward of New York was favored to win the presidential nomination. Among the minor candidates was Illinois' favorite son, ex-congressman Abraham Lincoln. On May 18, the day the balloting was to begin, Seward's followers paraded through the downtown streets, waving banners and singing victory songs. Meanwhile, the Lincoln people were at work. They printed up counterfeit admission tickets to the Wigwam and packed the spectator stands, shutting out the rest of the public. Now, during the speeches, whenever Lincoln's name was mentioned, cheers rocked the building. The enthusiasm seemed to have an effect on uncommitted delegates. Though Seward led the first roll call, on the third ballot, Lincoln was nominated. In November, he was elected president. And Chicago had begun to establish its reputation for hardball politics.

May 19, 1903

First Ward alderman Michael Kenna, better known as "Hinky-Dink," opened his new saloon at Clark and Van Buren today. The main room measured one hundred feet long by fifty feet wide, and Kenna boasted he now had "the largest barrel house in the world." The bar itself was fully eighty-four feet long. On the second floor, the alderman had provided lodging for two hundred men, with private lockers and shower baths available for one-dollar-a-week rent. "I'm going to give these poor hobos the best home they've ever had in their life," Kenna told a reporter. Of course, the lodgers were expected to vote the proper way whenever an election rolled around. And the barrelhouse itself promised to be a real moneymaker. One of Kenna's friends estimated the business would earn a first-year profit of $100,000—double the salary of President Theodore Roosevelt.

May 20, 1991

On this date, Washington Square Park was added to the U.S. National Register of Historic Places. That's the official name and the name in the guidebooks. Chicagoans know the little square across from the Newberry Library as Bughouse Square. During the 1890s, the park became a popular place for orators to exercise their free speech rights. Since most of their causes weren't mainstream—and since a "bughouse" was another name for an insane asylum—the police began calling the place "Bughouse Square," and the name stuck. The soapbox tradition continues in the park each July, with the Newberry's annual Bughouse Square Debates.

May 21, 1924

On May 21, 1924, thirteen-year-old Bobby Franks disappeared while walking home from school in the Kenwood neighborhood. The next morning, his wealthy parents received a ransom note. Before any money could be paid, Bobby's body was found in a remote area near Wolf Lake. Police also found a pair of eyeglasses they traced to nineteen-year-old neighbor Nathan Leopold. The young man said he'd been out with his buddy, eighteen-year-old Richard Loeb. Questioned separately, their alibis broke down, and both of them confessed to the killing, though each said the other had done the actual deed. Why had two rich young intellectuals murdered the boy? They said they had wanted to commit "the perfect crime." In court, Clarence Darrow argued that Leopold and Loeb had diseased minds, saving them from the hangman. The murder of Bobby Franks became the subject of dozens of books and two movies and is often called Chicago's Crime of the Century.

May 22, 1987

The papers called it "the Lake Forest Chainsaw Massacre." Actor Laurence Tureau, better known as Mr. T, was using a chainsaw to cut down dozens of trees on his North Shore estate. Word was that Mr. T was allergic to trees. Neighbors agreed that Mr. T was friendly to kids and was cooperative with local zoning authorities. They just wished he was a more thoughtful landscaper. The next year, Lake Forest enacted a tree preservation ordinance.

May 23, 1996

The state legislature changed the name of the Calumet Expressway to the Bishop Ford Freeway today. The new name honored Louis Henry Ford (1911–1995), twice elected presiding bishop of the Church of God in Christ. Besides being the first Chicago expressway named for an African American, the Bishop Ford Freeway was also the first Chicago expressway to be called a "freeway." No reason was given for the innovation, so maybe it was simply chosen for alliteration.

May 24, 1920

Today, Chicagoans were shocked—shocked!—to learn that gambling was going on in the bleachers at Cubs' Park. Gamblers had staked out their own area of the stands, and anyone who wanted to get down a bet knew where to find some action. So with the cooperation of team officials, a squad of undercover cops infiltrated the open-air casino. Once the starting pitchers were announced, the betting began. During the first inning, the wagers came fast and furious on each pitch. A gambler would call out his offer— "A dollar he swings at the next pitch"—and somebody would take it. At the end of the inning, the undercover cops all stood up, and in one voice announced, "You're all under arrest." They herded forty-seven gamblers out of the bleachers, marching them the two blocks down Addison Street to the Town Hall Police Station. The accused men were booked and released on twenty-five-dollar bonds, pending court appearance. Presumably, the gambling in the ballpark bleachers was now ended.

May 25, 1981

Shortly after 6:00 a.m. this Memorial Day, security at the Sears Tower spotted someone in a Spiderman costume climbing up the side of the building. The fire department was called. By now, the climber had passed the twenty-fifth floor, and the crew chief rejected the idea of punching open a window to grab him. A deal was reached with the climber—he could finish his ascent, but would be attached to a lifeline, with a safety net deployed below. With that, the man resumed climbing. On the street below a crowd of about two hundred people had gathered to watch. At 10:25 a.m., the climber reached the top and was immediately arrested. The man in the Spiderman suit turned out to be Dan Goodwin, an acrobat in a Las Vegas lounge show. He said he was trying to publicize how hard it was to rescue people trapped in tall buildings. "Spider Dan" was soon released, without being charged.

May 26, 1934

The Century of Progress Exposition opened its second season today. The day was highlighted by the Dawn-to-Dusk Dash. The Chicago, Burlington & Quincy Railroad was showing off its sleek new train, the Pioneer Zephyr, with a nonstop run from Denver to Chicago. The trip normally took twenty-five hours, but the Zephyr would be trying to do it in a single day's daylight—dawn to dusk. The CB&Q had cleared the 1,015 miles of track, with grade crossings guarded by railroad employees and volunteers from the Boy Scouts. The Zephyr left Denver at 6:04 a.m. local time. Fifty miles out, the engineer eased the control handle up to 112 miles per hour. The train moved smoothly on, without a shake or rattle. Throughout the day, radio reports announced its progress. At 8:09 p.m. the Zephyr pulled into Chicago Union Station. The trip had taken thirteen hours, five minutes, at an average speed of seventy-seven miles per hour. The next day, the Zephyr was displayed at the Exposition grounds. From there, it went on a thirty-one-state publicity tour before being placed in regular service.

May 27, 1918

Theodore Roosevelt had challenged William Howard Taft for the presidency in 1912. That had split the Republican Party and handed the election to Democrat Woodrow Wilson. The two ex-presidents had been feuding since then. On May 27, 1918, the country learned that they'd patched things up in Chicago. Arriving at the Blackstone Hotel, Taft spotted Roosevelt sitting in the dining room with some other people. Taft walked up and stood behind Roosevelt. When Roosevelt's dinner companions suddenly stopped talking, he turned around to find Taft grinning at him. Roosevelt immediately jumped up, gave Taft a bear hug and began pumping his hand. Seeing this, diners at other tables got to their feet and applauded. Roosevelt found a place for Taft at his table. The two old friends spent the next half hour in animated conversation, then went their separate ways. Eight months later, Roosevelt died. Taft attended the funeral.

May 28, 1914

On this date, a bowling ball left Chicago for a trip around the world. The stunt was devised by the Brunswick-Balke-Collender Company to publicize its new Mineralite ball and was big news at a time when people didn't travel much. The idea was to ship the ball from one YMCA to another in the various British colonies scattered throughout the globe. And all started out fine. The Mineralite went from Chicago to San Francisco to New York to London to Paris to Berlin and—World War I broke out. When the strange object got to Berlin, the Germans were suspicious and sent it back to Paris. Brunswick came up with a new routing, and by November, the ball had arrived in India. A few weeks later, news reached Chicago that the ship carrying the Mineralite to Australia had sunk in the Indian Ocean. A few weeks after that, new news reached Chicago that the Mineralite had actually missed the doomed ship and was safe. The world-traveling bowling ball finally completed its journey in May 1915 and was proudly displayed at the Panama-Pacific Exposition in San Francisco.

May 29, 1949

With the weather getting warmer, many Chicagoans were heading for the corner of Diversey and Pulaski and Olson Rug Park. The rug company had created this North Woods–model oasis for its employees in 1935, and now it was open to the public, free of charge. The property had rock gardens, climbing paths, a duck pond, shrubs, trees and a waterfall. Before the park closed in 1978, over 200,000 people were visiting each year.

Olson Rug Park. *Author's collection.*

May 30, 1937

Workers at the Republic Steel Plant were trying to organize a union. On Memorial Day 1937, about 200 of them began marching across a field toward the plant. Some of the men had brought their wives and children along. Blocking the way were 150 Chicago policemen. Words were exchanged. Rocks were thrown. Tear gas was let loose. Clubs were swung. Shots were fired. The police charged. The strikers scattered. In the aftermath, 10 marchers were dead and over 60 injured. Police casualties number 40 injured. In American labor history, the incident has become known as the Memorial Day Massacre.

May 31, 1985

How well was CTA serving disabled riders? A group called Americans Disabled for Accessible Public Transportation (ADAPT) was trying to get hydraulic wheelchair lifts put on all new buses. CTA said the $15,000-per-bus cost would break the budget. On May 31, fourteen ADAPT members staged a protest on the State Street Mall. When a bus rolled up to the Madison Street stop at 11:30 a.m., the first disabled person lifted himself out of his wheelchair and slowly climbed up the steps. The process was repeated with other buses and other passengers. Some of the people took as long as seven minutes to board. When the demonstration ended, and bus traffic on State resumed its normal pace, both sides tried to put their own spin on the matter. CTA's spokesman said there was already a dial-a-ride service in operation and that the demonstrators "accomplished nothing other than to prove they know how to disrupt traffic." ADAPT countered that CTA was embarrassed and didn't want riders to know the truth. The Americans with Disabilities Act would become law in 1990 and address many of these problems.

June 1, 1960

To most Chicagoans in 1960, the Garrick Theater was a dingy Loop movie house. The owner wanted to tear it down, and today, the city building commission gave its approval. That decision sparked a battle. Built in 1894, the Garrick was a seventeen-story office tower with a 1,300-seat auditorium. It had originally been called the Schiller Building. Architectural historians considered the Garrick one of the finest works of Adler & Sullivan, and the city landmarks commission had listed it as one of thirty-six Chicago structures having "architectural importance." However, the designation carried no legal weight. Preservationists were outraged that this masterpiece was going to be leveled in favor of a parking garage and launched a protest. Demonstrators marched with "Save the Garrick" signs. Mayor Richard J. Daley refused to issue a wrecking permit, appointing a commission to study the matter. The owners responded by going to court, and the city was ordered to issue the permit. Early in 1961, the Garrick was demolished. But Chicago's historic preservation movement had begun.

June 2, 1927

Newly elected mayor William Hale Thompson signed an order today to relicense Chicago's five thousand soft drink parlors. During the past four years, Mayor Dever had pulled most of their licenses because most of the establishments had been caught violating the Prohibition law. Now that Thompson was back in the mayor's chair, he was following through on his campaign pledge to ease up on Prohibition enforcement. Many of the soft drink parlors had gone back into business anyway, and the police were wasting time enforcing morals when they should be busy catching crooks. The city was also losing an estimated $500,000 a year in license fees. Thompson's order appropriated $33,000 to hire thirty new collectors in the license department. A mayoral spokesman denied charges that the thirty new hires were mere patronage appointments and said the collectors would immediately begin a block-by-block licensing survey.

June 3, 1861

Senator Stephen A. Douglas died of typhoid fever on this date, at the age of forty-eight. He is best known to history as the second half of the Lincoln-Douglas debates of 1858. Little Steve beat Big Abe in the senatorial election that year but lost their presidential rematch in 1860. Locally, Douglas was a big booster of Chicago. He dreamed up the Kansas-Nebraska Act to get the South to support a Chicago-based transcontinental railroad. He also donated land near his lakefront estate for the first University of Chicago. Douglas has a Chicago neighborhood and a major West Side park named for him. That's his tomb off Lake Shore Drive at 35th Street.

June 4, 1913

Heavyweight boxing champion Jack Johnson was sentenced to 366 days in the Joliet penitentiary and fined $1,000 today. He'd been convicted of violating the Mann Act by transporting a woman across state lines for immoral purposes. The law was supposed to curb prostitution. But for the federal government of 1913, the big problem was that Johnson was black, and the woman he'd brought from Pittsburgh to Chicago was white. "This defendant is one of the best known men of his race," the judge said. "His example has been far reaching." Johnson was allowed to remain free on $30,000 bail while his conviction was under appeal.

June 5, 1955

Fifty couples renewed their vows in the tower room of the Conrad Hilton Hotel this Sunday morning. The occasion was a special "Wedding Bells" ceremony held each year by Reverend Kenneth Hildebrand of the Central Church of Chicago, which conducted its services at the hotel. All the couples had been joined in matrimony by Reverend Hildebrand in the course of his twenty-three-year ministry. The first couple he married in 1932 was there. So was a couple married just yesterday, who'd delayed their honeymoon a day. A lady came all the way from Tennessee with her two small children, despite her husband being called away by work at the last minute. Reverend Hildebrand told the couples to be unselfish, to appreciate each other and to put religion to work in their home. Summing up, he said that a happy marriage was like "a long conversation that always seems too short."

June 6, 1892

On this date, the Chicago L began service. Operated by a private company named the Chicago & South Side Rapid Transit, the trains ran from Congress south to 39th Street. Unlike New York—where the elevated trains ran over public streets—the Chicago L right of way was in the alley between State and Wabash, earning it the nickname the Alley L. The coaches were pulled by steam locomotives. Patrons bought five-cent tickets from an agent in the ground-floor station, climbed up the stairs to the platform and gave the tickets to another agent. Today's revenue service began at 7:00 a.m, when a northbound train left 39th Street. On board the four coaches were thirty passengers. After stopping at eight intermediate stations, Chicago's first Monday rush hour train pulled into Congress terminal at 7:14 a.m., right on time. The new service was a success, and construction was soon underway to extend the line to Jackson Park for the upcoming Columbian Exposition.

June 7, 1958

America had an estimated five thousand drive-in movie theaters in 1958, and Chicago had its share. On this Saturday night, the most popular outdoor movies were *Macabre* and *Hell's Five Hours*. This double feature was playing at the Sunset, the Harlem Avenue, the Skyhi, the Halsted, the Route 41 and the 66. The Bel-Air on 31st Street and the Double Drive-in on Western Avenue were both showing the two horror movies on one of their screens, while presenting Elizabeth Taylor in *Raintree County* on the other. For patrons wishing to stay within the chiller genre but looking for something different, the 95th Street Starlite had a triple feature—*Brainless Creature*, *The Weird Wolf* and *The Devil Comes*. Meanwhile, the North Avenue in Melrose Park bucked the horror trend by showing a comedy double, *Merry Andrew* and *The Road to Bali*. In 2014, all of these drive-in theaters are gone.

June 8, 1869

Chicago inventor Ives McGaffey received a patent for the world's first vacuum cleaner on June 8, 1869. McGaffey called it a "sweeping machine," and it contained all the elements of a modern model—except the electric motor. While pushing the device along the carpet, the user had to turn a hand crank to suck in the dirt. Fortunately, these early vacuum cleaners were lightweight, constructed out of wood and canvas. McGaffey's device was manufactured by the American Carpet Cleaning Company of Boston under the named the Whirlwind. List price was $25, the equivalent of $450 in 2014 money. Only two examples of the original McGaffey vacuum exist, most having been lost in the Great Chicago Fire of 1871.

June 9, 1930

Just after 1:30 in the afternoon, *Tribune* reporter Jake Lingle was walking through the busy tunnel under Michigan Avenue at Randolph, when a man came up behind him, shot him once in the back of the head, then got away in the crowd. Chicago newspapers were outraged. Rewards totaling $55,000 were offered by the *Tribune* and its rival papers. The whole city seemed to turn out for the fallen reporter's funeral at Our Lady of Sorrows Church. Then, bit by bit, certain facts began to come out. Lingle was making sixty-five dollars a week but had lived like royalty. He kept a suite at the Stevens Hotel, took vacations in Cuba and was driven around by a chauffeur. He was friends with Al Capone, Bugs Moran and other gang lords. He was also close to the chief of police. Was Lingle a bagman arranging payoffs from the underworld to crooked cops and politicians? A small-time hood was eventually convicted of the murder, served a light prison sentence, then disappeared. More than eighty years later, the killing of Jake Lingle remains a mystery.

June 10, 1922

The *Chicago Tribune* celebrated its seventy-fifth anniversary by announcing a unique contest. Planning to move from the Loop to North Michigan Avenue, the paper invited architects to submit designs for its new headquarters. A prize fund of $100,000 was being offered for "the most beautiful building known to men." More than 260 entries were eventually received. First prize of $50,000 went to John Mead Howells and Raymond Hood. The neo-Gothic structure based on their entry was completed in 1925 and continues to serve as the *Tribune* headquarters.

June 11, 1920

The year 1920 looked like a Republican year. Whoever was the nominee at the Chicago convention would likely be elected president. Among the many candidates was Senator Warren G. Harding of Ohio. Though Harding was considered a longshot, his campaign manager predicted that the convention would deadlock, and on the fourth day, the party bosses would gather in a "smoke-filled room" at the Blackstone Hotel to select a compromise candidate—namely, Harding. The reporters who heard the outrageous prediction could barely keep from laughing. But sure enough, that's the way it worked out. The major candidates knocked each other off, the bosses met behind closed doors on the fourth day and Harding became the Republican nominee. He was elected president in November by a landslide. And in our own time—even with all the restrictions on smoking—we still call a private gathering of political fixers a "smoke-filled room."

June 12, 1991

The Chicago Bulls won their first National Basketball Association championship today. They defeated the Los Angeles Lakers 108–101, to take the final playoff series in five games. The Bulls and the Lakers had met in the playoffs four times in the past, with the Lakers winning each time. But now the Bulls had Michael Jordan, and that made the difference.

June 13, 1927

Vernon Cooley, a Michigan Avenue dentist, had been paying his ex-wife, Margaret, fifty dollars a month for alimony. He wanted to be relieved of the burden because Margaret was now engaged in "riotous living." Today, the Appellate Court turned down his petition. The judges said that Margaret's post-divorce behavior had no bearing on the question of alimony—and besides, she'd obtained the divorce on the grounds of Vernon's infidelity. Vernon Cooley was not pleased with the decision. A *Tribune* report said he was forming an organization of divorced men dedicated to combating "gold digging ex-wives."

June 14, 1948

The Philadelphia Phillies were staying at the Edgewater Beach Hotel while in town for a series at Wrigley Field. First baseman Eddie Waitkus was making his first trip to Chicago after being traded away by the Cubs. About 11:00 p.m., he received a note that a young woman wanted to see him. Waitkus went to her room. When he got there, the woman produced a rifle, told Waitkus he'd been bothering her for two years and shot him in the chest. The sound brought people rushing to the room. Waitkus was badly wounded and rushed to the hospital. The shooter was nineteen-year-old Ruth Ann Steinhagen. Though she'd never met Waitkus, Steinhagen had become obsessed with him and thought killing him was the only way to relieve her tension. Waitkus survived to continue his baseball career. Steinhagen was found to be legally insane, was committed to a mental institution and was released after receiving shock treatments. The Edgewater Beach incident later became the basis for the novel (and movie) *The Natural.*

June 15, 1937

This was the day Carl Hansberry moved his family into the three-flat he'd bought at 6140 South Rhodes Avenue. Hansberry was a black man moving into an all-white neighborhood. That evening, two bricks smashed through the front window, and police posted a guard around the property. Two days later, six of Hansberry's neighbors filed a $100,000 suit against him in circuit court. The three-flat had been under a restrictive covenant, which said it could only be sold to whites. Restrictive covenants were common, and the court ordered the family to move. Hansberry fought back, appealing the decision. The case finally made its way to the U.S. Supreme Court. In a unanimous decision, the high court ruled in Hansberry's favor on November 13, 1940. However, the Supreme Court ruled only on the merits of the particular case, and restrictive covenants were not declared unconstitutional until 1948. Carl Hansberry was dead by then. But years later, his youngest daughter, Lorraine, became the celebrated author of *A Raisin in the Sun*.

June 16, 1900

A group of North Side businessmen was asking the city council to replace cable cars with electric trolley cars. Cable cars currently operated on Clark, Wells and Clybourn. Fully two-thirds of the men surveyed favored electric cars. Though the cost would be over $1 million, the Chicago Union Traction company said it would convert its lines, if that's what the public wanted. Mayor Carter Harrison Jr. also supported modernizing the street railways. However, the mayor felt that downtown Chicago was already too cluttered with overhead wires, and the new electric lines should operate with an underground trolley, as in New York and Washington, D.C.

June 17, 1812

John Kinzie and Jean Lalime were two civilian settlers living near Fort Dearborn. Once friends, they had become bitter enemies. On the evening of June 17, as Kinzie walked near the fort, Lalime came after him with a pistol. They went at it hand-to-hand. Kinzie was shot in the shoulder, but Lalime got the worst of it—he fell on his own knife and died. Lalime was popular with the garrison, so Kinzie's friends spirited him away until tempers cooled. The killing was ruled self-defense. Kinzie returned to live out his life as Mr. Pioneer Settler. According to one story, Lalime's soldier friends buried his body near Kinzie's cabin, so Kinzie would always be reminded of the killing. In 1891, a skeleton was unearthed near the corner of Cass (Wabash) and Illinois. Though the remains were possibly Jean Lalime, no definite identification could be made. At last report, the skeleton was in the custody of the Chicago Historical Society.

June 18, 1857

Mayor John Wentworth was used to getting his way. Part of the reason was that he stood six feet, six inches tall. In the spring of 1857, he'd been elected mayor on a platform of "cleaning up" Chicago. Sometimes the cleanup was literal. Laws were on the books saying that merchants couldn't clutter the city's wooden sidewalks. The laws had been ignored. Storekeepers hung awnings and signs over the public walk or cluttered it with display cases. If the offender were given a citation, the case would take months to go through court and then might be tossed out by a friendly judge. On the evening of June 18, the mayor took direct action. He sent his police out to tear down any obstruction blocking the public sidewalk. The junk was collected in wagons and dumped into a pile at the public market, where the owners could retrieve it. The merchants complained, but Wentworth had public opinion on his side. The sidewalks remained uncluttered.

June 19, 1975

In 1945, rising young hoodlum Sam Giancana purchased a brick bungalow in suburban Oak Park. He continued to live in the house as his daughter grew up, his wife died and he became top man in the Chicago Outfit. In 1965, he was jailed for refusing to testify before a grand jury. He moved to Mexico after his release but kept the Oak Park house. In 1975, the feds brought him back home for further questioning. On the evening of June 19, 1975, Giancana was in the basement of the Oak Park house, frying sausage and peppers at a stove, when someone shot him in the back of the head. The murder was never solved. Though Oak Park currently has three historic districts and dozens of historic buildings, there are no plans to designate the Sam Giancana home an official village landmark.

June 20, 1976

During the 1950s, Clayton Moore became famous playing the Lone Ranger on TV. Moore was a native Chicagoan who'd attended Senn High School before dropping out to enter show business. In 1976, *The Lone Ranger* program was still being shown in reruns, and Moore was still doing public appearances in costume. On the evening of June 20, he checked in at the Lincolnwood Hyatt. His van was too big for the regular lot, so he was told to park it outside. The next morning, Moore found that the van had been broken into and several items stolen, including an antique gun valued at $1,200. The loot was never recovered. The newspapers had a lot of fun with the story, noting that on TV the bad guys never got the drop on the masked man. But then, the Lone Ranger had never been to a Chicago suburb.

Lincolnwood Hyatt, later The Purple Hotel. *Photo by the author.*

June 21, 1893

The Ferris wheel was invented by a man named George Washington Ferris. He got the idea from the Eiffel Tower, the hit of the 1889 Paris Exposition. Now that Chicago was staging its own World's Fair in 1893, Ferris wanted to outdo the French. Bicycles were a new fad, so Ferris was going to construct a gigantic, rotating bicycle wheel. He convinced investors to back him to the tune of $400,000. On June 21, the Ferris wheel was ready. The structure was three hundred feet high and had thirty-six shed-like cars that could hold sixty passengers each. For fifty cents a rider got two spins on the wheel, which lasted twenty minutes. From the first, the public loved the big wheel. On a clear day, you could see all the way to Wisconsin or across the lake to the Michigan shore. By the time the fair closed in October, nearly 1.5 million people had ridden the first Ferris wheel.

June 22, 1918

This was the date of the Hammond circus train wreck. Just before dawn, a Michigan Central train plowed into the rear of the Hagenbeck-Wallace Circus train just east of Hammond. The cars in the circus train caught fire, and sixty-one people were killed, most of them as they slept. The Michigan Central engineer said the warning semaphore he went through had been obscured by steam. The victims' remains were buried in a mass grave in the Showmens Rest section of Woodlawn Cemetery in Forest Park.

Showmens Rest in Woodlawn Cemetery, Forest Park. *Photo by the author.*

June 23, 1911

Chicago bootleggers were in the news today—for selling margarine. The dairy industry had convinced politicians to restrict the sale of the butter substitute, and Illinois had strict margarine laws. Inspectors from the state food commission had identified six Chicago businesses trying to pass off margarine as butter. One accused lawbreaker was a door-to-door salesman who'd made the mistake of selling margarine to an inspector's wife. Citing the Pure Food and Drug Act, margarine critics claimed it was an unsafe food. Federal officials weren't entirely convinced by this argument; they just wanted to make sure the margarine excise tax was paid. Two "margarine moon shiners" had been convicted in Judge Kenesaw Mountain Landis's court. The men each drew eighteen-month sentences in the federal prison at Leavenworth. The message was unmistakable—fake butter would not be tolerated!

June 24, 1926

The Twenty-eighth International Eucharistic Conference of the Catholic Church was coming to Chicago for five days in June 1926. An outdoor Mass was scheduled for St. Mary of the Lake Seminary in the village of Area. Anticipating the event, the village board voted to change the name of Area to Mundelein, in honor of George Cardinal Mundelein. The cardinal was so pleased he donated a new fire truck to his new village. On June 24, 1926, an estimated half million people drove cars or took special trains to the renamed village for the Mass and closing ceremonies.

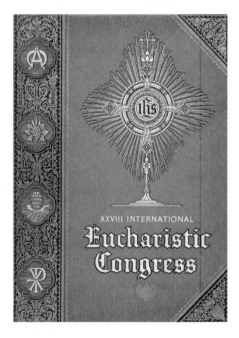

Program from the 1926 Eucharistic Congress. *Author's collection.*

June 25, 1916

After two years of construction, Chicago's Municipal Pier was finished. The 3,300-foot-long pier was the longest in the world, planned to serve both commercial shipping and recreation. Known as Navy Pier since the 1920s, the facility was put to various uses, including serving as the Chicago branch of the University of Illinois. An extensive renovation in the 1990s transformed the pier into Chicago's number one tourist attraction.

Municipal Pier, now known as Navy Pier. *Author's collection.*

June 26, 1954

A seiche is a large wave that rolls through a lake because of sudden changes in air pressure or a seismic disturbance. Chicagoans learned the definition on this Saturday morning. A storm squall near the southeastern end of Lake Michigan caused a five-foot wave to rise near Michigan City around 8:00 a.m. Moving west and growing larger, the seiche hit Chicago at 9:30 a.m. By then, it was at least ten feet high. Fishermen on the piers at North Avenue and Montrose Avenue were suddenly swept into the water. "I've been coming to the lake since I was a kid and I never saw anything like it," one fisherman said. "It was just as if somebody put giant hands into the water and pushed it up into my face." As quickly as it had come, the seiche passed on, leaving eight drowning victims behind it.

June 27, 1942

He was a twenty-two-year-old naturalized American citizen, a graduate of Schurz High School who'd belonged to ROTC. Then he'd gone back to his native land, been radicalized and returned to America a terrorist, planning to blow up military installations. He was Herbert Hans Haupt. He was born in Germany. And now it was 1942, World War II was on and Haupt was one of eight Nazi saboteurs arrested by the FBI on June 27. The feds nabbed Herbie behind the wheel of his new Pontiac near the Webster Avenue L station. President Franklin D. Roosevelt ordered the eight men tried by military tribunal as "unlawful combatants." Haupt claimed he'd been trapped in Germany when the war started and had joined the sabotage team so he could get back to America. The court didn't accept that. All eight defendants were convicted, and six of them—including U.S. citizen Herbie Haupt—died in the electric chair on August 8, 1942.

June 28, 1956

Today, the world's first privately owned nuclear reactor went into operation at the Illinois Institute of Technology. Twenty-four industrial firms had joined with IIT to fund the $750,000 project nicknamed "the atomic furnace." Before the device was turned on, project director Haldon Leedy briefed reporters. Leedy said there was no danger of a radiation leak, since the furnace was made of concrete five feet thick and had numerous other safeguards. Because of a special containment system, there would be no air pollution. Nuclear energy was a cheap, endless source of power. Radiation could also be used to sterilize food and perhaps even in the fight against cancer. With Leedy's briefing concluded, one of the scientists sat down at a control panel outside the reactor room and began flicking switches. On the other side of a plate glass window, behind two airlock doors, the atom furnace began humming. An alarm bell clanged. Overhead, a signal light flashed the words: "REACTOR ON."

June 29, 1947

The body builders were in Chicago for the annual Mr. America competition. Thirty-nine men flexed and posed at the Lane Tech auditorium. When it was over, the title was awarded to twenty-one-year-old Steve Reeves of Oakland. An army veteran of World War II, Reeves had started developing his body three years earlier. Now he had 212 pounds of muscle on his six-foot, one-inch frame and sported a twenty-nine-inch waist with a fifty-one-inch chest. The *Tribune* noted that most of the audience at the competition was female, and when Reeves was announced as the winner, his name "drew sighs that were almost screams." After winning the Mr. America crown, Reeves became an actor. His most famous role was starring as Hercules in two high-grossing Italian films.

June 30, 1925

You'd been hearing the idea more and more lately. In 1925, Chicagoans were talking secession. The Illinois Constitution said that legislative districts had to be redrawn every ten years, after the U.S. census. That hadn't been done since 1901. Downstaters controlled the legislature and didn't want to give Chicago more power. According to Alderman John Toman, the city deserved five more state senators and fifteen more state reps. The solution was for the city to split off from the rest of Illinois and form a new state. The proposed State of Chicago would take in all of Cook County. With 3 million people, that would rank it eleventh among forty-nine states, giving it significant clout. Besides, as a state Chicago would be guaranteed two U.S. senators. Could the rest of Illinois be convinced into letting Chicago go? Probably not at this time. Yet the idea was worth exploring.

July 1, 1935

This evening the first of sixty-four free summer concerts was presented in Grant Park. Late afternoon rain probably cut down attendance, and fewer than four thousand people came out to the new band shell off 11th Street. They heard an opening program mixing old favorites from Wagner and Johann Strauss with selections from American composers. In his introductory remarks, Mayor Kelly thanked musicians' union president James Caesar Petrillo—also a member of the park board—for helping make the concerts possible.

Concert at the first Grant Park Band Shell. *Author's collection.*

July 2, 1932

The Great Depression was into its third year with the country's mood drifting into hopeless. In July, Democrats met in convention at the Chicago Stadium and nominated New York governor Franklin D. Roosevelt for president. The custom was for the nominee to be formally notified in a small ceremony at a later date. Roosevelt knew he'd been nominated and thought waiting to be told was ridiculous. He sent word that he was coming to Chicago immediately by plane—a dramatic gesture in an age when air travel was still a novelty. Arriving at the stadium on the evening of July 2, he accepted the nomination with a call to get the country moving again. "Millions of our citizens cherish the hope that their old standards of living and of thought have not gone forever," he concluded. "I pledge you, I pledge myself, to a new deal for the American people." That November, Roosevelt was elected president. His recovery program became known by the phrase he'd used at the Chicago convention, the New Deal.

July 3, 1894

George Pullman had created a model town for the workers at his railroad sleeping-car plant south of the city. But when the 1893 depression caused Pullman to reduce wages, he refused to slash rents or prices at his company store. In May 1894, his workers went out on strike. The American Railway Union backed the action, and soon sympathy strikes were spreading, tying up railroad traffic throughout the nation. On July 3, after several violent incidents and with the national economy paralyzed, President Grover Cleveland called out the army to get the trains moving again. He said he was trying to keep mail delivery on schedule. The Pullman Strike soon collapsed.

July 4, 1909

A group of prominent businessmen had commissioned architect Daniel Burnham to draw up a comprehensive blueprint for Chicago's future growth. On this Fourth of July, Burnham published his *Plan of Chicago*. The lavishly illustrated 164-page book called for lakefront parks and a landscaped boulevard system, straightening the Chicago River, improved railroad terminals, a regional highway network and a central cultural center. Burnham's plan was officially presented to the city two days later. Public reaction was enthusiastic. Before the year was over, the city council approved creation of a Chicago Plan Commission to oversee future implementation of Burnham's vision.

July 5, 1956

CTA was going to war. The enemy: pigeons. The birds had been a nuisance at L stations for decades. CTA had been trying to get rid of them but was hampered by city laws, which said that pigeons couldn't be shot, poisoned or otherwise hunted. The Anti-Cruelty Society had also been watching how the transit agency dealt with the birds. Now CTA had called in the professionals. A St. Paul company, Twin Cities Pigeon Eliminating, was given a contract to do some pigeon eliminating. Twin City's method involved traps baited with enough pigeon food and water to keep the birds comfortable until they were collected. The pigeons were then gassed. This was considered a humane method of disposal, since some exterminators sold the captured birds to gun clubs for target practice. Twin City's traps were being set up in five Loop L stations, as well as at the Wilson Avenue and the Cottage Grove–63rd stops. About the only person objecting to the program was Jerry Scalzo, owner of a hat-cleaning service on Wabash Avenue. "What are they trying to do?" he asked. "Ruin my business?"

July 6, 1933

The All-Star baseball game began as a special adjunct to the 1933 Chicago world's fair. Some sources say the idea came from Mayor Ed Kelly. Whether or not this is true, the legman who made it happen was *Tribune* sportswriter Arch Ward. Ward convinced the two league presidents to back the idea, then helped talk the few recalcitrant team owners into line. The *Tribune* agreed to guarantee the game against loss, and its staff tabulated the votes of the fans, who were picking the starting lineups. The two teams met at Comiskey Park on July 6, 1933. Babe Ruth, playing his twentieth season and slowing down, rose to the occasion. Maybe Chicago inspired him. Nine months after his "called shot" home run on the North Side, the Babe hit the first All-Star game home run on the South Side. The American League won, 4–2.

July 7, 1967

An alewife is a type of herring, about seven inches long. If you went to a Chicago beach during the 1960s, you knew about this fish. In those days, Lake Michigan was packed with alewives. Each summer the alewives died, and their bodies drifted to shore. The millions of dead fish stunk up everything, besides attracting millions of flies. Tractors and bulldozers were used to clean up the mess. The situation got so bad that *Time* magazine published a story about Chicago's annual alewife die-off on July 7, 1967. During the 1970s, experts determined that the alewife population had gotten out of hand because its natural predator—the trout—had been killed off by a bigger predator, so the government began putting salmon in the lake to dine on the alewives. Problem solved!

July 8, 1986

Jimmy Carter and his wife, Rosalynn, were in Chicago this week, volunteering at Habitat for Humanity. The ex-president was part of a team constructing a four-unit building in West Garfield Park. Carter said the project had given him and his wife "a new dimension in our lives." The Kildare Avenue building was finished on schedule, with the new residents happily moving in. In later years, it became derelict, and it was torn down in 2010.

July 9, 1893

Dr. Daniel Hale Williams was one of the country's first African American surgeons. In 1891, he founded Provident Hospital as the first black-owned and operated hospital. On this date a patient named James Cornish was brought into Provident with a knife wound in his chest from a barroom brawl. Cornish was near death, so Williams tried something radical, opening the man's chest and working on the beating heart itself. Williams didn't have X-rays, antibiotics or modern anesthesia. He performed the operation, saving the patient's life. Fifty-one days later, Cornish walked out of the hospital. Depending on which reference source you consult, Williams had performed either the first or second successful pericardium heart surgery in the United States.

July 10, 1896

The Democrats were meeting at the original Chicago Coliseum to pick a presidential candidate. The economy was bad, and the Free Silver wing of the party thought inflating the currency would speed recovery. On July 9, various delegates gave speeches on the issue. William Jennings Bryan, an ex-congressman from Nebraska, was one of the Silver speakers. What he said wasn't anything new—it was how he said it. Bryan was young and handsome, had a rich voice and knew how to give a speech. Two minutes into his oration, many of the delegates were applauding. As he went on, the applause came more often and grew louder. Then he concluded with imagery from the Bible, "You shall not press down upon the brow of labor this Crown of Thorns! You shall not crucify mankind upon a Cross of Gold!" With that, the delegates went wild. The next day, thirty-six-year-old Bryan became his party's presidential candidate. He campaigned vigorously throughout the country but lost the election to William McKinley.

July 11, 1886

Privately erected statue of Captain George Wellington Streeter. *Photo by the author.*

Captain George Wellington Streeter was a cunning rascal with a little steamship. On this day, he ran the craft into a sandbar off Superior Street in a storm. He couldn't move, so he stayed there and lived on board. As the years passed, builders dumped debris into the marshy lowlands around the sandbar, connecting it to the shore. Now Streeter, a Union army veteran, claimed the man-made land as his homestead. Squatters arrived and built shacks on the captain's 186-acre claim. Streeter himself had a keen eye for public relations, portraying himself as a little guy fighting the big-money fat cats who said they owned the land. There were raids, counterraids and lots of litigation through the 1890s, 1900s and 1910s. In 1918, Streeter was arrested for peddling liquor without a license. A little later, the courts finally decided against him and in favor of the big-money fat cats. Captain Streeter died broke a few years later. In our own time, the area of his old domain is proudly called Streeterville.

July 12, 1979

When he was the voice of the White Sox, Harry Caray used to tell listeners, "You can't beat fun at the old ball park." This was one time the fun got out of hand. The Sox were hosting a Disco Demolition Night at Comiskey Park. Anyone who brought a disco record was admitted for ninety-eight cents, and about fifty thousand people showed up. The highlight of the evening was supposed to be radio DJ Steve Dahl exploding a crate of disco records at home plate between games. But once Dahl blew up the records, a few fans jumped onto the field. Thousands more soon followed, overwhelming the security guards. The crowd tore up sod, knocked over the batting cage, pulled down banners and lit small fires. Announcer Caray and Sox owner Bill Veeck took turns on the public address system, trying to get everyone back into the stands. A police riot squad finally cleared the field, and the Sox forfeited the second game. In the years since, Disco Demolition Night has become Chicago's Woodstock—*everybody* claims they were at Comiskey that historic night.

July 13, 1912

In 1909, U.S. senators were chosen by the legislature of each state. That year the voting in Springfield took ninety-five ballots. The surprise winner was Congressman Billy Lorimer, a Republican wheeler-dealer from Chicago's West Side known as the Blond Boss. Lorimer took his senate seat in June. Months later, the *Tribune* revealed that one legislator admitted being paid $1,000 to vote for Lorimer and said that others had been bribed as well. Lorimer demanded the Senate investigate the charges. A committee was formed, came to Illinois, held hearings, confirmed there'd been bribery in Lorimer's election—but cleared him because he hadn't known about it! The full Senate voted to let Lorimer keep his seat. Time passed, and new bribery allegations surfaced. A second committee cleared Lorimer. But by now, the senator was becoming an embarrassment to his party. On July 13, 1912, the U.S. Senate voted to expel Blond Billy, 55–28. The next year, the Seventeenth Amendment to the U.S. Constitution turned Senate elections over to the people.

July 14, 1966

"All my friends are dead! I'm the only one alive!" Today, the quiet Jeffrey Manor neighborhood awoke to the frantic screams of twenty-three-year-old nursing student Corazon Amurao. She'd shared an apartment on 100th Street with other students. Now eight of them had been murdered. The night before, a young man with a gun had forced his way into the apartment. He smelled of alcohol and said he needed money to get to New Orleans. The nine nurses decided it was best not to resist. The intruder gagged them and tied their hands behind their backs. One by one, he led each of them into the next room. Meanwhile, Amurao rolled under a bed and hid. When the man was gone she crawled out, pushed open the door and stumbled over the eight bodies. Now police questioned the survivor and got a good description of the killer. Within days, they arrested Richard Speck. He claimed he'd been high the night of the murders and didn't remember anything. He eventually admitted to the crimes. Because of a Supreme Court ruling, Speck escaped the death penalty and died in prison in 1991.

July 15, 1933

Shortly after 6:00 p.m. General Italo Balbo and his fleet of twenty-four seaplanes landed in Lake Michigan near Navy Pier. The Balbo Air Squadron had flown to the Century of Progress Exposition on a goodwill trip from Rome, a journey that had taken two weeks because of stormy weather and an accident along the way. During the next three days, the general and his fliers were feted with a Soldier Field rally, speeches, banquets and assorted civic honors. Seventh Street was renamed Balbo Drive. The hoopla was later spoofed by the Marx Brothers in their movie *A Night at the Opera*. The next year, on the first anniversary of Balbo's visit, the City of Chicago accepted an ancient temple column as a gift from the Italian government. The Balbo Column was erected in the park east of Soldier Field, where it remains to this day.

July 16, 2004

Millennium Park was supposed to be finished in the year 2000, to celebrate the turn of the millennium. Four years later, it finally opened. The cost was $475 million, three times the original estimate. Still, the twenty-four-acre section of Grant Park was impressive, with the Bean and the Crown Fountain and the Pritzker Music Pavilion and all. One visitor was reminded of the public square in a European city. Mayor Richard M. Daley was confident his park would become a tourist attraction. "They talk about the Sears building, they talk about the Picasso, they talk about the Art Institute, the lake, the river," he said. "Now they'll talk about Millennium Park."

July 17, 1995

Chicago's great heat wave of 1995 began on Wednesday, July 12, when the temperature at O'Hare reached 98 degrees. Thursday's high was 106, a new record. Friday wasn't much better, at 102. By now, the city had set up eleven cooling stations, and though the program was widely publicized, few people were showing up. Every air conditioner seemed to be running at full speed, and the strain on the grid was causing widespread power outages. Meanwhile, the county morgue was overwhelmed with heat-related deaths. Refrigerated trailers were pressed into service to store the backlog of bodies. Saturday the high reached only 99, bringing hope that the worst might be over. On Sunday morning the mercury climbed to 94, hovered there, then slowly dropped. Monday, July 17, saw highs in the low 80s, marking the end of Chicago's five days of hell. The death count was estimated at seven hundred.

July 18, 1901

Alderman John Minwegen was riding over the Clark Street bridge in his buggy when he noticed two planks were missing from the roadway. He stopped his team and went looking for the bridge tender. He finally found the bridge tender's assistant. The man was surprised anybody would worry about a hole in the bridge. Minwegen called for a couple of planks, a hammer and nails. While a small crowd watched, he took off his coat and proceeded to personally repair the hole. The alderman was experienced in making repairs with wood—he owned a furniture store.

July 19, 1933

One of the big hits of the 1933 World's Fair was Sally Rand, a young fan dancer. Rand's act consisted of walking on stage nude, holding two giant fans made of ostrich feathers in front of her naked body and waving them around as she strutted to the tune of a classical music piece. Though the audience couldn't see much of Rand's body, the premise was daring for 1933. Someone had sued to stop Rand's performances as a threat to public morality. Today, the papers announced the decision by Judge Joseph B. David. The judge said he considered Rand's patrons "a bunch of boobs," but that wasn't a reason to stop her act. "We have the boobs, and we have a right to cater to them," the judge declared. He dismissed the suit, ruling that Sally Rand could continue her fan dancing.

The Century of Progress Exposition— "Which way to Sally Rand?" *Author's collection.*

July 20, 1924

Today, a Chicago swimmer became the sensation of the Olympic Games in Paris. Twenty-year-old Johnny Weissmuller was known to practice swimming laps around Goose Island in the Chicago River. He'd starred on the Illinois Athletic Club swim team for three years. Now, Weissmuller won the gold medal in the 100-meter men's free style in a world record 0:59:0. He finished a full one-second ahead of Duke Kahanamoku, for over ten years considered the world's greatest swimmer. Weissmuller also won a second gold medal as part of the U.S. men's relay team. In his career, he would eventually collect five Olympic gold medals and never lose a competitive race. He later became the movies' most famous Tarzan.

July 21, 1919

Employees at the Illinois Trust and Savings Bank on La Salle Street were just finishing up for the day. Twelve hundred feet overhead, the Wingfoot Express blimp was going through some practice runs when the hydrogen in one of its gasbags exploded. The blimp fell and crashed through the skylight of the bank. A few of the blimp's crew managed to parachute to safety. Two passengers weren't as lucky and were killed. In the bank below, nine more people died.

July 22, 1934

In the summer of 1934, John Dillinger was America's Bank Robber. Handsome and charming, he'd become a national celebrity. It didn't seem to matter that Dillinger and his associates had killed over twenty people. Dillinger claimed he was sticking it to the rich bankers and never stole from everyday people. When the cops did catch him, he'd bluffed his way out of jail with a wooden gun. Now, he was hiding in Chicago with a lady. On July 22, the FBI was tipped off that Dillinger would be attending the late show at the Biograph Theatre. The informer was Anna Sage, who was going along with the Dillinger couple. That evening, sixteen FBI agents and Chicago cops staked out the Biograph. When the movie let out, they spotted Sage's reddish-orange dress in the crowd. Dillinger saw them closing in and ran into an alley. Before he could get his gun out, he went down in a hail of bullets. John Dillinger died on the way to the hospital. Soon afterward, his fans were in the alley, sopping his blood off the pavement with handkerchiefs.

July 23, 1910

People didn't have hand-held electronic devices to pass the time while they rode the L to work in 1910. The Northwestern Elevated Railroad decided to make the journey more interesting with a contest to honor beautiful gardens. Any floral display visible from the L tracks was eligible. Cash was awarded for backyard gardens, window boxes and porch displays, with a first-place prize of fifty dollars in each category. The winners were announced on July 23. Nobody was surprised that one of the awards went to Mathias Overton of Sheffield Avenue—he'd taken home the grand prize in a 1908 *Tribune* garden contest. Mrs. J.P. Hutchinson of Winthrop Avenue was delighted to win because her husband had told her she was foolish to enter. Another happy winner was Reverend Paul Roberts of St. Joseph Catholic Church for an arrangement of geraniums, pansies, Zanzibar beans and other plants. The 1910 L Beauty Show seems to have been a one-time-only affair. Too bad.

July 24, 1915

On this bright Saturday morning, the steamship *Eastland* was moored at the south bank of the Chicago River, just west of Clark Street. The ship was getting ready to take 2,500 passengers to Michigan City, most of them Western Electric employees on their way to a picnic. When boarding began, the ship began listing. That wasn't unusual, and the crew corrected it, though some listing continued. Shortly after 7:30 a.m., the *Eastland* cast off. A few minutes later, it rolled over on its side and sank into the mud. The ship was barely twenty feet from the dock, and its hull jutted above the water line. Help was soon on the scene, but 848 people died. The sinking of the *Eastland* remains the single deadliest disaster in Chicago history. Nearly a century later, the debate goes on over just what caused it.

July 25, 1925

Even in 1925, brides were looking for ways to make their weddings distinctive. Dorothy McGonigie was set to marry Hartley Berglund, a student aviator. That gave Dorothy the idea of staging Chicago's first airborne wedding. At 1:00 p.m. this July 25, the two planes in the bridal party took off from the new flying field at 97th and Western. A crowd of two thousand people waited on the ground. The planes climbed to five thousand feet and then began a long glide downward. In the first plane, the bride and groom stood before Reverend Fred Line of St. Paul's-on-the-Midway Church and were joined in marriage, with the best man and maid of honor handling the rings. The second plane flew above, allowing the two flower girls to drop red roses on the newly married couple. When the planes returned safely to earth, Reverend Line could joke that now he really was a "sky pilot."

July 26, 1914

"Constituent service" was the name of the game for Third Ward alderman Jacob Lindheimer. The Chicago Beach Hotel was operating a private beach for its guests off 51st Street. Neighborhood residents wanted access, but the alderman was advised that nothing could be done until the courts rendered a decision. So Lindheimer paid a visit to the hotel's manager, and presto!—half of the beach was thrown open to the public. The episode was just another part of a Chicago alderman's daily routine, one for the voters to remember when the next election rolled around.

July 27, 1919

A hot summer afternoon in Chicago. A black teenager named Eugene Williams was swimming in the lake with friends off 26th Street. Williams drifted over toward the segregated beach reserved for whites. A white man on the beach threw rocks at Williams and hit him on the head or scared Williams so much he couldn't come ashore—the narrative is unclear here. What did happen for sure is that Eugene Williams drowned. When the police arrived and arrested a black man instead of the white rock-thrower, that infuriated the black swimmers. A fight broke out. Rumors spread. The South Side erupted in a race riot. Chicago's Mayor Thompson was feuding with Illinois' Governor Lowden and said the National Guard wasn't needed. Four days of bloodshed and burning went on. The mayor finally asked for the guard, and peace was restored. Five hundred people had been injured and thirty-eight were dead in the country's worst race riot to date.

July 28, 1955

Construction on the Congress (Eisenhower) Expressway was well underway. CTA planned to replace the Garfield Park L line with trains running up the middle of the expressway median. Today, that work would begin at Pulaski Road. Mayor Richard J. Daley arrived, descended onto the unfinished highway and walked across to the unpaved median strip. The mayor took off his coat in the ninety-degree heat. He grabbed a sledge, raised it over his head and pounded a spike into a railroad tie. Cameras clicked and spectators cheered. The ceremony over, Daley told reporters that the Congress project signaled "a new era in highway construction and mass rapid transit." He was right. When the line opened three years later, it was hailed as a practical innovation. Since then, many cities have combined transit lines and express highways.

July 29, 1850

Chicago had thirty thousand people in 1850. The city was becoming so big and sophisticated that an opera company came to town. Actually, the "opera company" was made up of four professional singers who were traveling through the Midwest performing Bellini's *La Somnambula*. For the July 29 Chicago debut, local talent filled out the rest of the parts. The amateurs rehearsed diligently, but opening night at Rice's Theatre had problems. Actors missed cues and wandered on stage at the wrong time. Whenever one of the hometown players appeared, friends in the audience would stand up and cheer. An extra named James McVicker sang so loudly he drowned out the other singers. Yet when the curtain finally rang down, all the confusion and mistakes were forgotten. Chicago had staged its first opera, and the whole town considered it a rousing success. The next night, during the second performance, Rice's Theatre burned to the ground.

July 30, 1970

Today, the city was looking for someone to buy the Southmoor. The three-hundred-room hotel at 67th and Stony Island was owned by an anonymous bank trust. Over the last six months, the building had been taken over by a local street gang. Management had unknowingly hired

The Southmoor before demolition, 1976. *Photo by the author.*

a few gangbangers, who then proceeded to scare off other employees. That made running the hotel impossible. "Elevator companies and plumbing contractors refused to service the building," the property manager said. "Their men were robbed or pushed around." Honest tenants had moved out, with monthly rent collection falling from $35,000 to $8,000. Two weeks earlier, a housing court judge had ordered the hotel vacated. Two companies were reported to be interested in the property.

July 31, 1927

Motorists were crowding gas stations this evening, trying to beat the new state tax of two cents per gallon going into effect at midnight. A gallon of gas was selling at sixteen cents, so the tax of more than 10 percent was pretty steep. Gas station attendants noted that customers were telling them, "Fill her up," instead of settling for five or ten gallons of fuel. The Chicago Motor Club had filed a complaint that the tax was discriminatory and unconstitutional. However, with the state poised to collect an estimated $15 million a year in revenue, the legislature had enacted the tax anyway. The oil companies said there was no plan to add another penny onto their prices to cover the cost of administering the tax.

August 1, 1950

The city's health experts were urging all Chicagoans to get tattoos. The Soviet Union had developed an atomic bomb, the Korean War was raging and the Chicago Civilian Defense Committee painted a grim picture of what might happen if the Bomb were dropped on the Loop. Dr. Andrew Ivy said that a nuclear blast would kill 61,000 people outright and injure 231,000. In such an event, emergency blood transfusions would be necessary. Treatment would be easier if a victim had a tattoo identifying blood type. Dr. Ivy suggested that the best place for this tattoo would be below the left armpit, an area that would likely be protected from the blast. However, Dr. Henrietta Herbolsheimer, the only woman on the committee, said that future fashions in women's clothing were difficult to predict, so a location on the inside of a leg might be better. The committee said that a list of facilities where the public might obtain the medical tattoo was being developed.

August 2, 1858

In Chicago's early days, organized volunteer fire companies handled the task of putting out fires. Rivalries between the companies developed, and sometimes two crews meeting en route to a blaze would forget about the fire and start at each other with fists and clubs. The volunteers didn't always do an effective job of putting out fires, either. In October 1857, a building on Lake Street burned down with a loss of twenty-three lives, leading to calls for a corps of paid, professional firefighters. The following year, the city council voted to disband the volunteer companies. The Chicago Fire Department was established on August 2, 1858.

August 3, 1929

Today, Chicago police launched its lake patrol. Two officers were sent out in the department's new speedboat. Noisy boats had become a nuisance, and the cops were going to stop it. The city's jurisdiction extended three miles out into Lake Michigan. Craft with loud outboard motors would be ordered to move past the boundary or be fined. The lake patrol would also be enforcing safety rules—just last week, a crash of two boats off Navy Pier had left two people dead. A request for three more patrol boats was before the city council.

August 4, 1940

In the largest antiwar rally Chicago had yet seen, over forty thousand people were at Soldier Field to hear an address by Colonel Charles Lindbergh. Fighting in Europe had been going on for eleven months now. Many Americans thought the country should become involved in the struggle to stop Nazi Germany's aggression. Lindbergh didn't agree. The great aviator was an isolationist and wore the label proudly. The important thing was that America keep its own defenses strong rather than waste resources on foreign adventures. "In the past we have dealt with a Europe dominated by England and France," Lindbergh told his audience. "In the future, we may have to deal with a Europe dominated by Germany." The speech was broadcast on a nationwide radio hookup. From Chicago, Lindbergh moved on to other cities with his message. He continued to draw enthusiastic crowds almost to the day the Japanese attacked Pearl Harbor and plunged the United States into World War II.

August 5, 1966

Dr. Martin Luther King Jr. had brought the civil rights movement to the cities of the North. Today, he was leading a march down 63rd Street in the Marquette Park neighborhood, protesting segregated housing. Opponents of open housing had gathered for their own demonstration. As King got out of his car at 63rd and Sacramento, a rock sailed through the air and knocked him to the pavement. Some of his friends told him to get back in the car for his own safety. King refused to hide. As he began the march, an angry crowd lined the sidewalk behind police lines. They threw rocks, bottles, firecrackers, chunks of concrete and at least one knife at King's group. Though they tried to break through to get at the marchers, the cops held them back. The day ended with thirty people injured and forty-one under arrest. "I have never seen anything so hostile and hateful as I've seen here today," King told his supporters.

August 6, 1912

Theodore Roosevelt had retired from the presidency after the 1908 election. Four years later, he wanted his old job back. He had won most of the primaries and still been denied the nomination by the Republican bosses. So on August 6, Roosevelt and his followers were at the Chicago Coliseum for the first convention of a new party, the Progressives. Roosevelt accepted their nomination with an hour-long speech. At the end, he brought the audience to its feet, comparing the current fight to the Bible's final war of good against evil—"We stand at Armageddon, and we battle for the Lord!" Roosevelt told a reporter he felt as fit as a bull moose, and Progressives soon became known as the Bull Moose Party. Despite a vigorous campaign—and despite surviving an assassination attempt—Roosevelt lost the election.

August 7, 1908

The Chicago & North Western Railroad today announced plans for a new terminal on Madison Street. The $20 million structure, including elevated approach causeways, would occupy four city blocks. The only larger rail terminal in the country was Boston's South Station. The C&NW's old Wells Street terminal was simply too small for the times. When construction on the Madison Street "pile" was completed in two years, railroad officials said it would be able to handle over a quarter million passengers every twenty-four hours.

Chicago & North Western Railroad Terminal. *Author's collection.*

August 8, 1988

The first night game in major-league baseball was played in 1935. By 1950, all the teams played night games—except the Cubs. Longtime owner Phil Wrigley said the national pastime was meant to be enjoyed in daylight. When the Tribune Company bought the Cubs in 1981, management began talking about putting lights in Wrigley Field. The neighborhood didn't like that and pressured politicians to pass laws banning night games at the ballpark. But night games made more money, and now it was only a question of time until the Cubs installed lights. A compromise was reached, where the number of night games would be strictly limited, and nonresident parking would be prohibited on nearby streets. On August 8, 1988, the Cubs met the Phillies in the first night game at Wrigley Field. Naturally, the park was a sellout on that historic 8-8-88. Just as naturally for something involving the Cubs, things didn't work out as planned. A major storm drenched the area, and the game was called after three innings.

August 9, 1953

George S. May owned a Chicago business-consulting firm. He also sponsored high-paying professional golf events at Tam O'Shanter Golf Course in Niles. May was a master promoter who saw great potential in television. On August 9, 1953, his World Championship became the first nationally televised golf tournament. The conclusion was memorable, in more ways than one. Lew Worsham came to the final hole needing a birdie three to tie for first place. After putting his drive in the middle of the fairway, Worsham hit a wedge 110 yards to the elevated green. The ball landed, rolled, rolled and went straight into the cup for a winning eagle two. This was too much for golf pro Jimmy Demaret, doing the TV color commentary. "How about that?" he shouted on-air. "The son-of-a-bitch went in!"

August 10, 1907

Essanay Studios was Chicago's pioneer movie studio, founded on this date. The name reflected the partnership of businessman George Spoor ("S") and actor Bronco Billy Anderson ("A"). Originally located on the Near North Side, Essanay moved to larger headquarters on Argyle Street in Uptown in 1908. Charlie Chaplin was the studio's biggest star, though he shot only one film in Chicago. In 1914, local teenager Gloria Swanson was "discovered" after visiting the Argyle Street studio with her aunt. Essanay was eventually absorbed by other studios.

August 11, 1966

The Beatles, the British rock quartet, were launching their third American tour. Today, they were in Chicago practicing damage control. Beatle John Lennon had been quoted in a British magazine saying the group was more popular than Jesus and predicting that Christianity would vanish. His remarks had led to protests in the United States and other countries and threats of concert cancellations. With the whole Beatles money-machine in jeopardy, Lennon was forced to apologize. At an Astor Towers press conference, he claimed he'd been misquoted. He had never said that the Beatles were better than God or Jesus or Christianity but had only been commenting on the secular nature of England. "I'm sorry for the mess I made," Lennon said. "I never meant it as an anti-religious thing." With that the press conference moved on to music matters, and the Beatles tour went forward as planned.

August 12, 1987

Ancient bones had been discovered during a construction excavation in Romeoville. The Illinois Archeological Survey dated them as being about 1,800 years old. Scientists had another piece to add to the puzzle of how people of the past had lived. "It appears that this was a fairly tough, hard, and strenuous life," one archaeologist said. "Just surviving was a constant struggle. You froze in the winter and fried in the summer. You grew your own food or you hunted for it, and sometimes the animals came hunting for you. If the wolves and the bears didn't get you, then a disease would. If you made it to 40, you were considered old."

August 13, 1946

The 1946 polio season had reached its peak and seemed to be winding down. This summer had been particularly brutal. Chicago had seen 153 cases and five deaths so far. In the suburbs, the numbers to date were 63 cases and four deaths. Dr. Edward Piszczek, director of the county board of health, said the cool weather was helping arrest the number of new cases. Meanwhile, Lyons was beginning to kill its fly and mosquito pests. The Des Plaines Valley Mosquito Abatement District planned to spray the entire village with DDT.

August 14, 1928

Ben Hecht and Charles MacArthur were two Chicago newspaper reporters trying to earn a little extra money. Following the old advice "write about what you know," they wrote a play about Chicago newspaper reporters. *The Front Page* opened on Broadway on this date. The play covers a single day at the old Cook County courthouse on Hubbard Street. Characters are based on people the authors knew in Chicago, and the plot echoes the bizarre 1921 jailbreak of Terrible Tommy O'Connor. The fast action and snappy dialogue clicked with both critics and theatergoers. The *Front Page* became one of the big hits of the 1928–29 Broadway season. It was later made into a movie three times and remains one of the plays most often performed by amateur theatrical groups. And until science perfects a time machine, *The Front Page* is one of the best ways to get a feel for what Chicago was like in the 1920s.

August 15, 1967

At noon, fifty thousand people had gathered in Civic Center Plaza and the surrounding streets. Chicago was unveiling its newest piece of public art, a gift to the city from celebrated artist Pablo Picasso. Mayor Richard J. Daley pulled the cord, the cover dropped way,

The Chicago Picasso. *Photo by the author.*

and there it was! But what was it? The untitled sculpture was fifty feet high, made of Cor-Ten steel to match the building behind it. Depending on whom you asked, it looked like a woman, or a bird, or a robot, or Bullwinkle the Moose. The whole thing weighed 162 tons. Picasso had refused a fee for his design, and most of the $350,000 construction cost had been paid by private donations. In general, the professional critics liked Pablo's gift. Public reaction was mixed. Alderman John Hoellen, whose ward included Wrigley Field, thought a fifty-foot-high statue of Ernie Banks would have been a better addition to the plaza. With the passage of time, most Chicagoans have accepted "The Picasso" as just another whimsical part of the city's tapestry.

August 16, 1960

In 1960, Charlie Weber was alderman of the Forty-fifth Ward. For Chicago's kids, the more important fact was that Charlie owned a piece of the Riverview amusement park. Each summer, he staged a gigantic "Charlie Weber Kids Day" where all the future voters were given the run of the place. Charlie himself used to walk through the happy throng passing out silver dollars. So the news of how he'd died this August 16 came as quite a shock. The night before, the alderman had come home late from a political meeting. He'd pulled his car into the garage attached to his ranch house, then likely fell asleep and had been killed by carbon monoxide from the car engine. The fumes had seeped into the house and killed Mrs. Weber, too. Charlie Weber was sixty-six years old.

August 17, 1918

The Industrial Workers of the World, a radical union headquartered in Chicago, had opposed the United States' entry into World War I. In April 1918, 101 IWW members went on trial in the federal courtroom of Judge Kenesaw Mountain Landis, charged with violating the recently enacted Espionage Act. The prosecution accused them of such things as resisting the draft, advocating industrial sabotage and conspiring with the enemy. The defense claimed that the government was making wild accusations in an attempt to break the union. The trial ended on August 17. It took little more than an hour for the jury to find the defendants guilty on all counts. They were given heavy fines and prison terms ranging up to twenty years. Big Bill Haywood, one of the IWW leaders, jumped bail and fled to the Soviet Union. In 1919, the U.S. Supreme Court upheld the Espionage Act, though some of its more extreme provisions were later repealed.

August 18, 1955

In 1955, Chicago police were on the biggest manhunt since the days of Dillinger. Richard Carpenter, a suspect in sixty robberies, had been a fugitive for eighteen months. Carpenter sightings were reported almost daily. Then, on August 16, Carpenter killed a police detective who'd tried to arrest him on a subway train and got away. The next evening, another cop spotted the fugitive in the Biltmore Theater on Division Street. There was gunfire, and Carpenter again escaped. While a citywide search went on for Cop-Killer Carpenter, he broke into a two-flat on Potomac Avenue, holding the family hostage. But on the evening of August 18, one of the hostages slipped out and contacted police. The two-flat was surrounded, searchlights filled the sky, a helicopter hovered overhead, two thousand people crowded Potomac Avenue—and it was all broadcast live into Chicago living rooms on the new medium, television. As the bullhorn blared the order for Carpenter to give up, he tried to escape by jumping into the window of the apartment next door. There was more gunfire, but this time, the police got their man. As Carpenter was led away, the crowd shouted, "Kill him! Kill him!" He was convicted of murder and executed in 1958.

August 19, 1948

American Airlines Flight 383 was on the last leg of a New York–Chicago trip when pilot Eddie Cycon discovered the front wheels would not descend. He radioed Midway traffic control. After consultation, Cycon was advised to set down at Glenview Naval Air Station, which had the best emergency facilities. Cycon spent an hour circling to burn off his excess fuel. Then he notified Glenview he was ready. The plane came in nose up, skidded down the runway throwing off sparks, then slowed to a stop. The five emergency doors opened, and the passengers slid down nylon ropes to safety. Within two minutes, the plane was empty. There were no injuries, and pilot Eddie Cycon was hailed as a hero. Stewardess Agnes Mae Vaughn was also praised for her calm, professional performance. Only Vaughn knew how much effort that had taken—American 383 had been her first flight.

August 20, 1922

Walter G. McIntosh & Company was offering tours today of a new real estate development in suburban Berwyn. Located at Ogden and Oak Park Avenues, Berwyn Terrace was already supplied with gas, electricity and all utilities. Sewers and cement sidewalks were also in place. Though located beyond the city's border, Berwyn Terrace was only nine miles from the Loop, closer to the heart of the city than Rogers Park, 75th-Halsted or some other Chicago neighborhoods. A commuter station of the Chicago, Burlington & Quincy Railroad was only a few blocks from the development; so was a 320-acre forest preserve. Home sites were being offered for as little as ten dollars a month. Persons wishing to inspect Berwyn Terrace would be provided transportation to and from McIntosh's Loop office.

Berwyn Terrace ninety years later— bungalow heaven. *Photo by the author.*

August 21, 1915

African Americans were moving north in what history has called the Great Migration. In 1915, Jesse Binga was already on his way to becoming Chicago's leading black banker. Today, his ad in the *Broad-ax* announced that his bank was paying 3 percent on savings accounts and that safe deposit vaults could be rented for three dollars a year. Binga's real estate department handled the buying or selling of property on commission, as well as managing estates for nonresidents. All services were available at the Binga Bank, located at the southeast corner of State Street and 36th Place.

August 22, 1950

Mayor Martin Kennelly today ordered a crackdown on jitney cabs operating on South Park Way and other nearby boulevards. The jitneys were carrying groups of up to six passengers at a time, charging fifteen cents per person. Though this was more expensive than the current twelve-cent CTA fare, it was significantly less than the meter rates on licensed cabs. The jitneys were breaking the law, and the mayor warned that drivers operating without a taxi license would be arrested. The Park District would also be holding public hearings on how to deal with this problem on its boulevards.

August 23, 1904

Gymnasiums would be included in six new schools being built on the South Side. That was the proposal put forward by a Board of Education subcommittee today. Modern educational philosophy said that schools should train children physically as well as mentally. Adding gym rooms was a necessity to keep up with the times. Local experts said that when the full board formally approved the plan, it would mark "a new era" in Chicago public education.

August 24, 1816

Several different documents called the Treaty of St. Louis were signed by the U.S. government and various native tribes. The one that interests us was dated August 24, 1816. In this treaty, the Potawatomi and two allied tribes gave up claim to the land that eventually became Chicago. The United States got a twenty-mile-wide strip of land, extending southwest from points ten miles north and ten miles south of the Chicago River's mouth. Well into the twentieth century, many city maps continued to identify each diagonal as an Indian Boundary Line. Rogers Avenue and Forest Preserve Drive follow the northern boundary line.

August 25, 1956

Frank Lloyd Wright had never liked skyscrapers or what they represented. Now America's most famous architect had changed his mind. On this date, he announced plans for a grand building in Chicago that would top off at 5,280 feet—literally, a mile high. Dismissing skeptics, Wright said he'd already interested several backers for "The Illinois" and had selected a lakefront site near the planetarium. Most of the tower's 528 floors would be office space for city, county and state government. The top nine floors were for TV studios, topped off by a 330-foot antenna for coast-to-coast broadcasts. As many as 100,000 people could be accommodated in the building. With a total floor area of 18 million square feet available for rent, the tremendous construction costs could be earned back in a short time. The eighty-nine-year-old architect was clearly excited about the project and continued to talk it up six weeks later, when he arrived in Chicago with a twenty-two-foot-tall sketch of his skyscraper. However, "The Illinois" was still nothing more than talk when Wright died in 1959.

August 26, 1968

One of Chicago's more memorable political conventions opened on this date. The Democrats were meeting at the International Amphitheatre. The country was deeply divided by the Vietnam War. Though President Lyndon Johnson had already announced he was stepping down, the convention promised to be a magnet for protesters. Mayor Richard J. Daley was determined that any protests would be orderly, and the Chicago police were ready, as was the Illinois National Guard. On the third day, as Hubert Humphrey was nominated for president, the smoldering tensions between protesters and cops ignited. TV viewers saw violent scenes in Grant Park of police chasing and beating civilians. The protesters said that the authorities were out of control. The cops and guardsmen said the protesters had provoked them so much they feared for their own safety. Back at the amphitheater, Mayor Daley was shown on camera shouting an angry response to a speaker who'd accused the cops of "Gestapo tactics." The Democrats left Chicago a badly shattered party, and Humphrey lost the election. The city would not host another national political convention until 1996.

August 27, 1922

On this date, millionaire coal magnate Francis S. Peabody died of a heart attack on his Hinsdale estate. A few years later, the Peabody family sold the property to a group of Franciscan friars. Then the rumors began. There was a tiny chapel on the estate, and supposedly Mr. Peabody had been laid to rest there, floating inside a crystal casket like a DuPage County Lenin. This was just the sort of tale that appealed to teenage boys, and starting in the 1930s, whole generations of them went off in search of Peabody's Tomb, usually after dark. Traffic was heaviest around Halloween

Chapel on the former Peabody Estate. *Photo by the author.*

and during fraternity initiation season. All this disturbed the friars in their contemplation. Now, new rumors spread that trespassers were forced to pray on their knees all night and were whipped if they resisted. No one ever proved that the Franciscans had cooked up this later tale, though the number of unwanted visitors sharply declined. The property was eventually sold to the DuPage County Forest Preserve District and thrown open to the public.

August 28, 1994

Generations of Chicagoans thought of Maxwell Street not as a street but as an outdoor flea market. The first Russian Jewish peddlers began displaying their wares from pushcarts on Maxwell near Halsted during the 1870s. From there, it grew into a colorful, multiethnic bazaar sprawling in all directions over the nearby blocks. A prize-winning book (*Maxwell Street: Survival in a Bazaar*) and a prize-winning documentary film (*Cheat You Fair*) contributed to the legend. Then the University of Illinois began expanding southward. The old Maxwell Street was doomed. The last day was August 28, 1994. A more antiseptic version of the market continues a few blocks away.

August 29, 1893

Whitcomb Judson was a Chicago inventor. In 1889, he'd developed a type of streetcar that ran on compressed air. When that wasn't commercially successful, he turned to the problem of fasteners. Legend says he was tired of wasting time lacing up the high-top shoes then in fashion. Judson came up with a hook-and-eye system that was opened and closed by a sliding fastener. He called his invention the clasplocker. Though he first applied for a patent in November 1891, he did not receive formal approval until August 29, 1893. Soon afterward, Judson successfully exhibited the device at the Columbian Exposition and later founded the Universal Fastener Company to manufacture it. In our own time, Whitcomb Judson's clasp-locker is in common use under a different name—the zipper.

August 30, 1981

The name said it all: the Arlington Million. Arlington Park was hosting the first Thoroughbred horse race with a $1 million purse. The winner would earn $600,000, nearly double the top prize of the Kentucky Derby, and the final field of fourteen horses included entries from England, Ireland and France. Interest in Europe was so high that NBC added special satellite TV coverage of the race. Weather on the big day was pleasant, and 30,637 came out to Arlington to watch the action in person. The race itself turned out to be an exciting contest between favorite John Henry and a forty-to-one longshot named The Bart. Charging furiously at the end, John Henry finally came through to win by a nose. In the years since, the Arlington Million has become a major event on the racing calendar.

August 31, 1914

A great war had broken out in Europe, and the *Tribune* was determined to bring Chicagoans the latest play-by-play action. Today, the paper unveiled a giant war map on the Dearborn Street side of its building. The map showed the European continent, with the contending armies identified by color. As each new dispatch from the war zone arrived, the markers for the various army units would be moved to reflect the changing tide of battle. The movements of the warring navies were also being depicted by tiny ships of the appropriate colors. The *Tribune* war map would be illuminated at night, making it easily visible from a half block away.

September 1, 1921

An article in today's *Chicago Tribune* highlighted the liberation of American women. They were voting. They were driving cars. They were smoking in public. And they were getting rid of their corsets. "Women for the first time are giving their bodies a chance to develop naturally," said Dr. Katharine Corcoran. "Going without the corset is a good substitute for the old medicine ball." Of course, many women were not yet ready to abandon the corset. The newer models were being made from lighter-weight materials, so that they could be worn comfortably while still performing their function. The savviest manufacturers knew they'd have to adapt to the changing lifestyle of the modern female. As Dr. John Mahoney put it, "The women of the present day are paying more attention to their work and their sports, than they are to their hearts and their appearance."

September 2, 1919

Today, the city began a crackdown on polluters. The Steiner-Lee Dye Works was located at 823 East 39th Street. For over ten years, the plant had bothered the neighborhood with its soot and smell. During the past month, nine people had filed separate complaints with the city's health commissioner, Dr. John Dill Robertson. Warnings to Steiner-Lee management had been ignored. So now Robertson sent two inspectors to the factory, and the boilers were put out. A police guard was left on duty. In a statement to the press, the health commissioner noted that this was the first time a city factory had been closed because it was a smoke nuisance. He vowed to shut down any business that would not comply with the law. As their most basic right, Chicagoans deserved to have clean air.

September 3, 1984

When the Northwest (Kennedy) Expressway was being built in the late 1950s, the median strip was left empty. The plan was to extend the Logan Square L line to O'Hare Airport on the median. In 1970, trains did start running on the Kennedy, but only as far as Jefferson Park. There was talk that the Chicago & North Western Railroad was worried about losing commuter business and had blocked a farther extension. After Metra took over commuter service, work got underway on pushing the L through to O'Hare. In 1983, the line was extended to River Road in Rosemont. Finally, after twenty-five years of planning and building and waiting and building, CTA's "train to the plane" reached O'Hare on September 3, 1984. Mayor Harold Washington cut the ceremonial ribbon, and Dizzy Gillespie provided appropriate music on his trumpet: Duke Ellington's "Take the A-Train."

September 4, 1955

Emmett Till was a fourteen-year-old African American from Chicago killed by two white men in Mississippi. When Till's body was returned to Chicago, his mother insisted on an open casket. Over 200,000 people viewed the battered, mutilated corpse, many of them fainting at the sight. The publicity over the brutal murder of Emmett Till is seen as a turning point in the civil rights struggle.

September 5, 1918

The Cubs were opening the World Series against the Red Sox, using Comiskey Park because of its large seating capacity. In the seventh inning, the fans stood up for the customary stretch. World War I was being fought, and a military band began playing "The Star-Spangled Banner." A few in the crowd started singing along. Others joined in. By the time the song reached its climax, the entire ballpark was belting out the words. Then everybody cheered and applauded. The next day's newspaper accounts of the game reported the spontaneous demonstration, and soon, playing "The Star-Spangled Banner" became a regular feature of major athletic events. Congress made the song the official national anthem in 1931.

September 6, 1928

Today, workmen began the task of moving a ten-thousand-ton church. Our Lady of Lourdes Catholic Church had been erected on the southeast corner of Ashland and Leland Avenues in 1916. There, it sat peacefully for a dozen years. Then, the city announced plans

Our Lady of Lourdes Church at its latest location. *Photo by the author.*

to widen Ashland. Rather than tear down the beautiful Spanish Romanesque building, the pastor chose to have it moved to the other side of Ashland. Contractors were hired and the church jacked up off its foundation. Then, very slowly, fifty men, two tractors and several teams of horses began taking the building on its four-hundred-foot journey. Once it had crossed Ashland, the church was rotated ninety degrees to face Leland. The building was also cut into two parts and separated so that a thirty-foot-long extension could be slipped into the middle of the sanctuary. The move was completed in the spring, and Our Lady of Lourdes was rededicated on its new site in September 1929. Since that time, it has remained in place.

September 7, 1928

Antonio Lombardo was thirty-seven years old and listed his occupation as "wholesale grocer." He was also known to be a close associate of Al Capone. Today, Lombardo was gunned down at Dearborn and Madison, at the height of the evening rush hour, in front of hundreds of people, including two of his own bodyguards. Capone had recently helped Lombardo get elected president of the Italo-American National Union, a politically potent fraternal group. Police speculated that the killing might have been engineered by the disgruntled losing candidate. The two shooters got away in the crowd, and Lombardo's murder was never solved.

September 8, 1986

Oprah Winfrey came to Chicago in 1984 to take over as host of a local talk show on WLS-TV. *The Oprah Winfrey Show* went national on this date. The topic of the first broadcast was "How to Marry the Man or Woman of Your Choice." Winfrey and her program became tremendously popular over the course of the next twenty-five years, a cultural touchstone. The last show was broadcast in 2011.

September 9, 1915

In a meeting at the Wabash Avenue YMCA, Carter Woodson and four associates founded the Association for the Study of Negro Life and History. Part of their motivation was to counteract the racist portrayal of black Americans in the recent epic movie *The Birth of a Nation*. Nearly a century later, Woodson's organization continues its work as the Association for the Study of African American Life and History. Woodson himself is considered the Father of Black History. One of Chicago's regional libraries is named for him.

September 10, 1901

President William McKinley had been wounded in an assassination attempt on September 6, 1901. The shooter was an anarchist and told police he'd been inspired by Emma Goldman. Now, a nationwide hunt was on for the woman called the "high priestess of anarchism." Goldman had recently been seen in Chicago, and six of her associates were arrested. Meanwhile, police staked out her known haunts. On the night of September 9, Goldman was spotted entering a four-flat on Sheffield Avenue. The next morning the cops moved in. Goldman was arrested and went along quietly to the Harrison Street lockup. In less than an hour, newspapers were on the street headlining the capture of the most dangerous woman in America. Goldman steadfastly denied being part of any conspiracy to shoot the president. Since no evidence was found linking her to the crime, she was eventually released, as were her associates. McKinley died on September 14, and his assassin was executed six weeks later.

September 11, 1961

Bozo's Circus premiered on WGN-TV as a lunchtime kids' show on this date. Though other cities had their own programs featuring the franchised clown character, the Chicago version was the one that became most popular, especially after WGN became a cable "super-station" in the 1980s. The demand for studio tickets became so great—and the waiting list so long—that many Chicago women would send in their request as soon as they knew they were pregnant. The show ended its run in 2001.

September 12, 1967

Chicago police were dealing with a new scam today. A visiting conventioneer had gotten into a cab and told the driver to take him "where the action is." The driver responded that the best place was Pierre's Key Club, at 4200 North

The search for Pierre's Key Club. *Photo by the author.*

Clybourn Avenue, so they headed there. Except the address was bogus, and the conventioneer wound up at a dive in Cicero, where he had to fork over ten dollars for key club membership. But that wasn't why the man was now filing a complaint with the police. He'd paid one of the women at the club twenty-five dollars to come back to his hotel, and she never showed up! No doubt stifling some grins, the Chicago cops passed on the case as being out of their jurisdiction. The Illinois liquor commissioner eventually got the matter, with the result that a few Cicero taverns were shut down—for a while. And city cab drivers no longer touted the pleasures of Pierre's Key Club.

September 13, 1927

Fanny Brice, the beloved musical comedy star of the Ziegfeld Follies, was in a Chicago courtroom today, seeking a divorce. She'd married Nick Arnstein in 1918. A charming six-foot-six gambler and con man, Nick had spent a portion of their married years in prison on a stock swindle. Fanny had stood by him then. But things had started going bad once he was released. Fanny had gotten plastic surgery to straighten her nose, and Nick lost interest in her. When Fanny discovered Nick was having an affair, it was the end. Nick did not appear in court to contest the divorce, which was swiftly granted by Judge Otto Kerner Sr. Fanny was awarded custody of the couple's two children. She did not ask for alimony, saying that she was earning enough money on her own. Reporters had gathered outside the courtroom, and Fanny told them that she still loved Nick. When they tracked down Nick, he claimed that he still loved Fanny. In spite of their professed mutual love, Fanny Brice and Nick Arnstein lived separately ever after.

September 14, 1957

Winnetka is a picturesque, peaceful North Shore suburb. It's not the sort of place you'd expect to have a riot, particularly not during the serene *Leave It to Beaver* 1950s. Yet there was this riot. New Trier High School had just defeated Harrison High at the football stadium. One of the local kids snatched a football and was detained by school officials. That didn't go over well with the New Trier students. When a cop arrived to deal with the football thief, the kids began rocking his car. The officer called for help, and three more squads arrived. Meanwhile, over one thousand young people had gathered. Someone started tossing firecrackers. Then, the fire department arrived. They finally dispersed the mob by spraying a gentle mist of water into the air. Two students were arrested for disorderly conduct. The Great Winnetka Riot was over.

September 15, 1930

Milton Sills, one of Hollywood's most famous actors, died at his California home today. The forty-eight-year-old star of such epics as *The Sea Hawk*, *Miss Lulu Bett* and *Hard-Boiled Haggerty* was playing tennis with friends when he succumbed to an apparent heart attack. Born into a wealthy Chicago family in 1882, Sills graduated from Hyde Park High School, then entered the University of Chicago. While in college, he began appearing in campus productions. He received his BA in 1903 and was hired to teach mathematics by the university. Though Sills had planned to pursue a PhD, he decided instead to join a company of traveling actors. He eventually found his way to the Broadway stage. Success there led him to Hollywood in 1914, to appear in *The Pit*. A versatile performer who could play both muscular and cerebral roles with believability, Sills soon became a major silent-film star. He'd recently made the transition to talking films in *The Barker*, demonstrating that he would continue his career at the top. Sills often returned to Chicago to visit his family. His final resting place is Rosehill Cemetery in his native city.

September 16, 1936

Chicago was in the middle of the Depression but could still chuckle. Today's story involved a young Wisconsin farm girl named Hazel who'd come to the big city for a singing audition. On the bus she became acquainted with an older man named Mr. LaRue. LaRue said he was a Hollywood agent and might be able to get her into the movies, if she could demonstrate her figure was good enough for the cameras. Hazel arranged to meet LaRue at his room in the Morrison Hotel. Then she went to the police. Two detectives accompanied her to the hotel, waiting in the hall while Hazel kept her rendezvous. Inside his room, LaRue greeted Hazel warmly. He produced copies of official-looking studio contracts and a silhouette chart, took out a tape measure and told Hazel to get undressed. With that, Hazel gave a signal, and the detectives burst in. LaRue quickly confessed that he was not a Hollywood agent but a clothing salesman. His name wasn't even LaRue. As he was being led away to the police station, he explained: "Something snapped in my brain when I saw this girl on the bus, that's all!"

September 17, 1934

Six thousand teenage boys marched down the middle of Addison Street. They started at Wrigley Field and headed west. Carrying tiny American flags in their hands, they shouted and waved at the people lining the sidewalk. Behind the six thousand boys were squads of ROTC cadets and the bands from seven high schools. They were all going to the dedication of the new Lane Technical High School at Addison and Western. Student enrollment had outgrown the old Lane on Sedgwick Street, so the board of education had purchased part of the Mid-City Golf Course and built the world's biggest high school. Now the marchers reached the new campus and filed into the football stadium. They listened to various dignitaries give uplifting orations on the value of learning. They cheered when Mayor Ed Kelly told them, "I'm looking at you, and I see real men." The ceremonies ended and the students dispersed. Tomorrow was a school day. They'd have to get down to business then.

September 18, 1889

Jane Addams came from a wealthy family in northwest Illinois. She'd been impressed by the new concept of charity being developed in England, where concerned "social workers" would live among the poor people they wanted to help. In 1889, after inheriting a sizeable amount of money, Addams put her idea to work in Chicago. She spotted an old brick mansion that had seen better days on Halsted Street and convinced the owner to lease it to her rent-free—hence the name Hull House, after the owner's uncle. On September 18, Addams and her friend Ellen Gates Starr moved in. The idea of two well-bred, upper-crust young ladies setting up housekeeping in a notorious slum did seem strange, and on the first night, Addams left one of the doors wide open. When they woke up the next morning and found nothing missing, she took it as a hopeful sign for the future. The people of the neighborhood came to accept Adams and Starr. Within a short time, Hull House offered medical care, a dining room, a bathhouse, a library, a gymnasium, a night school for adults, lodging for twenty women and the city's first kindergarten.

September 19, 1911

Fourteen-year-old Charley Young was one of the thousands of runaways turning up in Chicago each year. A policeman had picked him up, barefoot and hungry, in Grant Park. Until a week earlier, Charley had lived with his grandfather, three brothers and one sister on a farm in Stanton, Missouri. His mother was dead, and his father had moved away with his new wife. Life on the farm had been all right until Granddad had told him to wash the dishes. That was "women's work," so Charley had hopped a freight to St. Louis and eventually made his way to Chicago. Now Charley admitted to being homesick. "Granddad was good to me but I didn't know it," Charley said, tears running down his cheeks. "I'd like to tackle a big stack of dishes right now if I was back in Missouri. I'm never again goin' to make a fuss, no matter what Granddad puts me at."

September 20, 1957

Today, Chicago got its own cop show on network TV, with the premiere of *M Squad*. The half-hour NBC drama was based on a mythical special unit that investigated all sorts of crimes, giving the writers plenty of story latitude. Lee Marvin starred as Lieutenant Ballinger. Marvin was a former combat marine who was just making his mark as an actor, and he was perfect as the no-nonsense Ballinger. The series ran for three years of popular and critical acclaim, then Marvin left to become a major movie star. A half century later, part of the fun of watching *M Squad* is picking out supporting actors who'd also go on to notable careers—Burt Reynolds, James Coburn, Angie Dickinson and Leonard Nimoy, to name a few. For Chicagoans, there's also a chance to see what the grittier parts of the city looked like in the late '50s. But don't try to find the police station used for *M Squad* headquarters. That building, at Racine and Superior, was torn down to make way for the Kennedy Expressway.

September 21, 1860

Chicagoans had their first look at royalty on this date. Albert Edward, Prince of Wales and heir to the British throne, had been touring Canada when he happened to meet Chicago mayor John Wentworth. The nineteen-year-old prince was intrigued by tales he'd heard about the city and accepted the mayor's invitation to visit. Though the trip was unofficial and unannounced, word soon got out, and over half the city showed up to welcome the distinguished visitor. The prince spent the day inspecting the courthouse, the water works, a grain elevator and other points of local interest, making appreciative comments. Then, he left the city, off to a country estate for some hunting. For his part, Mayor Wentworth thought the prince was a fine young man, royal or not. A reporter asked the mayor how it felt to sit next to a future king. "I didn't sit next to the prince," Wentworth said. "The prince sat next to *me*."

September 22, 1959

After forty years of frustration, the Chicago White Sox were on the verge of clinching the American League pennant. The decisive game in Cleveland was being telecast back to Chicago. At 9:41 p.m., CDT Sox shortstop Luis Aparicio fielded a ground ball, kicked second base for the force and then fired the ball to first for a game-ending double play, and a 4–2 victory. The Sox were going to the World Series! And now, all over the city, the air raid sirens were blasting. It so happened that Soviet leader Nikita Khrushchev was in the United States—maybe somebody had shot him, and World War III was underway. Of course, most baseball fans knew that the sirens were being sounded to celebrate the Sox. The next day, Fire Commissioner Robert Quinn took the blame for scaring the public with the false alarm. But there's still belief that the siren order had come from the city's number one Sox fan, Mayor Richard J. Daley himself.

September 23, 1991

Flight delays were plaguing O'Hare International Airport, and there were several competing solutions to the problem. Chicago mayor Richard M. Daley was in favor of building more runways at O'Hare. Others favored a third major airport, to go with O'Hare and Midway. Some people suggested expanding the little-used Gary Regional Airport. Another group wanted to build the new facility in a southwest exurb, Peotone. Daley himself had floated the idea of constructing a third airport in the city east on Lake Calumet, which would involve leveling the Hegewisch community. Almost forgotten was an earlier idea from an earlier Mayor Daley—Richard J. had once proposed putting Chicago's third airport on a man-made island in Lake Michigan. As of 2014, Chicago still makes do with just O'Hare and Midway.

September 24, 1969

The 1968 Democratic Convention in Chicago attracted thousands of protesters, most of them angry about the Vietnam War. Riots broke out in the city streets. Months later, eight activists were indicted on federal conspiracy charges connected with the disorders. Their trial began in the courtroom of Judge Julius Hoffman on September 24, 1969. It soon degenerated into farce. Judge Hoffman ran a tight ship, while the defendants saw the trial as an opportunity to publicize their different causes with outrageous behavior. One of them, Bobby Seale, was so disruptive the judge ordered him gagged, and his case was later separated from the others. Defendant Abbie Hoffman, no relation to the judge, insisted on calling him "Julie." Meanwhile, a new generation of protesters gathered outside the court daily, protesting the trial of the original protesters. The Chicago Seven trial ended on February 18, 1970. The defendants were found guilty on some counts, not guilty on others. At the same time, Judge Hoffman sentenced all seven defendants and two of their lawyers to jail time for contempt of court. All charges and sentences were later overturned in higher courts.

September 25, 1962

One of Chicago's more memorable championship boxing bouts took place on this date. The site was Comiskey Park. Floyd Patterson, the popular champion, was defending his title. Yet the champ entered the ring a decisive two-to-one underdog to opponent Sonny Liston, a very tough thug who'd already served two hitches in prison. Because Liston was supposed to have mob connections, the New York State Athletic Commission had refused to grant him a license, and so the fight had been moved to Chicago. The opening bell rang, and the boxers got underway. Spectators were still arriving when Liston caught Patterson with a left hook and dropped him barely two minutes into the first round. It was one of the quickest title knockouts in history. Legend says that Patterson was so embarrassed by his poor showing that he left Chicago disguised in glasses and a fake beard.

September 26, 1960

Presidential debates are relatively new. The very first one took place at the CBS Studios in Chicago on September 26, 1960. The Republican candidate was Vice President Richard Nixon, the Democrat was Senator John F. Kennedy. The topic was domestic issues. Each man made an opening statement, answered questions from four newsmen, rebutted any points his opponent had made, then gave a closing statement. The hour went quickly, and neither man made any gaffes. All three TV networks carried the debate, which attracted an audience of 70 million out of a U.S. population of 160 million. Conventional wisdom says that Kennedy "won" this first debate because he looked better on TV than Nixon. Whether or not this was really true, Kennedy moved ahead in the polls soon afterward and won a narrow victory in November. Though there were no debates during the next three presidential campaigns, they resumed in 1976. They've been with us ever since.

September 27, 1947

Chicago in 1947. *Author's collection.*

The Municipal Court of Cook County was under fire today. According to anonymous insiders, politics had taken over. All the administrative jobs, from the chief bailiff down to the lowliest clerk, were held through political connections. Lawyers complained that scheduling was handled through "a Chinese system of paying out small sums"—if you didn't take care of the clerk, your paperwork would be "lost." Cops said that cases were routinely dismissed if a defendant had clout. A majority of the thirty-six judges were doing an adequate job, but at least a dozen were totally incompetent. A few of them ran their courts like an assembly line, running through one hundred cases in the morning call so they'd have the afternoon free. And with the judge done for the day, members of his staff could work at a second job, or go to the racetrack. Municipal Court officials refused to comment on the accusations.

September 28, 1920

"Say it ain't so, Joe!" The little boy outside the county courthouse heard rumors that Shoeless Joe Jackson and other White Sox players had thrown the 1919 World Series and wanted Jackson to reassure him—but Jackson couldn't do it because he'd just confessed. The story of the tearful kid might have been made up. But eight Sox players were indicted this day for taking bribes from gamblers to dump the series, and team owner Charles Comiskey suspended them. The case dragged on into 1921, long enough for the players' confessions to disappear. When they finally went on trial, they were acquitted in two hours. Despite the acquittal, the eight "Black Sox" were banned for life from playing major-league baseball.

September 29, 1982

This morning, a twelve-year-old schoolgirl in Elk Grove Village awoke with a sore throat, took some Tylenol and collapsed. Paramedics were called, but the girl soon died. Later in the day, reports came in of three sudden deaths in an Arlington Heights family. Local authorities discovered that all three had taken Tylenol from the same bottle—and that the capsules had been tainted with cyanide. Now the death of the Elk Grove Village girl was also linked to the deadly medicine. Over the next three days, three more Tylenol deaths were reported, in Elmhurst, in Winfield and in Chicago's Old Town. Since the capsules had been manufactured in different places, that could only mean someone was sabotaging the bottles in stores. All Tylenol was pulled off the shelves, with three more poisoned bottles turning up. No more deaths were reported, and drug companies developed better ways of making their bottles tamper-resistant. A New York man was later arrested and convicted of using the deaths in an extortion attempt. However, Chicago's Tylenol murders remain unsolved.

September 30, 1927

William McAndrew had been hired as school superintendent in 1924 and told to clean up the system. While many of his reforms were applauded, he also antagonized the teachers' union and some powerful politicians. In 1927, newly elected Mayor William Hale Thompson decided to force an immediate confrontation with McAndrew. Thompson's Board of Education suspended the superintendent, charged him with insubordination and ordered a public "trial," which began on this date. McAndrew attended the first few sessions, pointedly reading a newspaper. Fed up with the political grandstanding, he finally walked out and didn't return. At length, the Board of Education found McAndrew guilty on March 31, 1928. By then, his term had already been over for two months.

October 1, 1932

Babe Ruth hit his most famous home run on this date at Wrigley Field. Ruth's Yankees were in town to face the Cubs in the World Series. When Ruth came to bat in the fourth inning of Game Three, the Cubs began yelling insults and trash-talking at him. The legend says Ruth responded by pointing at the center field bleachers and then hitting a homer to that exact spot—like a man playing pool, he'd "called his shot." Many years later, a fan's 8 mm movie of the game surfaced, confirming that Ruth did make some sort of gesture in the general direction of the bleachers. Whether or not he was pointing is still debated. The only certainty is that the Cubs lost the game and the World Series as well.

October 2, 1890

Modern mass transit came to Chicago on this date, when an electric streetcar began operating on the South Side. The city had been served by horse-drawn street railway coaches since 1859, and in 1882, cable cars came to Chicago. Electric streetcars drew power from an overhead wire strung along the tracks. The collecting pole on top of the car was known as a trolley, so the new vehicles were often called trolley cars. Today's first streetcar line ran on 93rd Street between Stony Island and South Chicago Avenues. By 1906, the electric streetcar had completely supplanted all the city's horse and cable cars.

October 3, 1967

Riverview opened in 1904 as a German shooting club and picnic grove on Western Avenue near Belmont. Soon, it grew into the Chicago area's largest amusement park. By the 1960s, the park had 120 rides, including 6 roller coasters, and attracted close to 2 million patrons each year. The 1967 season ended with a Mardi Gras on Labor Day, as usual. A month later, the announcement came that the Riverview property had been sold to developers for $6 million. The individual rides were either sold off or junked, leaving Chicagoans with decades to debate what was the best part of Riverview—the Bobs, or the Pair-O-Chutes, or Aladdin's Castle, or the Rotor, or the Shoot-the-Chutes, or…

October 4, 1949

In 1946, Preston Tucker launched his own auto company in Chicago. He leased the largest factory building in the world, the 475-acre Dodge Aircraft Plant at 76th and Cicero, and announced plans to produce the Car of the Future. And Tucker's first prototype certainly was sleek and sexy—"the kind of car Flash Gordon would drive," someone said. However, Tucker ran into production problems. Only fifty Tucker Torpedoes were built. As time dragged on, the Securities and Exchange Commission began investigating Tucker's stock sale. In June 1949, Tucker and seven associates were indicted in federal court on multiple counts of mail fraud, conspiracy and SEC violations. Tucker claimed he was innocent, saying the Detroit auto companies were using their clout to stop a potential rival. The trial began on October 4. That same day, the lease on Tucker's plant was cancelled, and the property reverted to the federal government. Three months later, the defendants were found "not guilty" on all counts. Preston Tucker was free but bankrupt, and he built no more cars.

October 5, 1979

The Chicago Public School system had closed for the day, labeling it a "historic event." Karol Wojtyla had visited the city three years before, as a Polish cardinal of the Catholic Church. Now he was returning as John Paul II, the first incumbent pope to visit the city. Thousands had lined his motorcade route from O'Hare the night before. Today, the dynamic fifty-nine-year-old prelate was off to visit two parishes, followed by a meeting with seminarians at Quigley South. The main event of the day was an open-air afternoon Mass in Grant Park, with an estimated 1.2 million people in attendance. The pope's final appearance was at a special Chicago Symphony Orchestra performance at Holy Name Cathedral. Then he was gone, after forty busy hours. The city later commemorated the whirlwind papal visit by renaming a portion of 43rd Street as Pope John Paul II Drive.

October 6, 1923

Edith Cummings of Lake Forest today won the women's amateur golf championship at Rye, New York. Though her play was erratic, the twenty-four-year-old "Fairway Flapper" was still able to defeat three-time champ Alexa Stirling on the thirty-fourth green. Cummings later became the first female athlete featured on the cover of *Time* magazine and was the inspiration for the character Jordan Baker in *The Great Gatsby*—though no one ever accused Cummings of cheating.

October 7, 1893

Today, the *Chicago Evening Post* published the first "Mr. Dooley" column by Finley Peter Dunne. Mr. Dooley was a mythical Irish bartender who dispensed wisdom in a thick brogue from his Archer Avenue saloon. His observations were often absurd and brought gut-shaking laughter, yet they always contained something to be pondered. Readers learned that Mr. Dooley spoke truth. Within a few years, Finley Peter Dunne's alter-ego was a national sensation. In 2014, his thoughts still have relevance. Mr. Dooley said, "The Supreme Court follows the election returns." Mr. Dooley said, "A newspaper comforts the afflicted and afflicts the comfortable." And perhaps reflecting his Chicago roots, Mr. Dooley said, "Trust everyone—but cut the cards."

October 8, 1871

The Great Chicago Fire started on a Sunday evening in a barn behind the O'Leary house, at what's now 558 West De Koven Street. There's no evidence it was caused by a cow kicking over a lantern. The fire quickly got out of control. Pushed by strong southwest winds, the flames spread to the business district, jumped the river and burned through the North Side. On Monday night, with a diminishing wind and a light drizzle, the fire burned itself out near Fullerton Avenue. Except for the Water Tower and three other buildings, everything in its path had been destroyed. About two hundred people had been killed. On Tuesday, Chicago began rebuilding.

The Great Chicago Fire of 1871. *Author's collection.*

October 9, 1906

The Chicago Cubs had won 116 games and lost only 36, breezing to the 1906 National League pennant. Over in the American League, the White Sox had barely edged out two other teams—with a .230 team batting average, the Sox had been nicknamed the "Hitless Wonders." The Cubs were clearly the stronger team. Still, they had each won their league championships and would face each other in the World Series. On October 9, a crowd of 12,693 people turned out at the Cubs' West Side Park to watch the opener. The first game of the first crosstown World Series ended with the Sox scratching out a 2–1 victory. It was a major upset, and so was the series. The Sox won in six games and became world champions. Since then, the Cubs and Sox have each been to the World Series a few times but have not faced each other. This raises a tantalizing question—which will Chicago get first, another crosstown World Series or the Olympic Games?

October 10, 1944

"$5,000 Reward for Killers of Officer Bundy on Dec 9, 1932." The notice appeared among the personal ads in the October 10, 1944 edition of the *Chicago Times* and gave a number to call. Intrigued by the listing, the city editor had a reporter investigate. It seemed the ad had been placed by Tillie Majczek, whose son Joe and another man had been convicted of killing the cop in a South Side speakeasy. Tillie had worked ten years as a scrubwoman putting together the reward. Now the reporter investigated further. He uncovered numerous irregularities in how the case had been handled. The *Times* printed a series of stories suggesting an innocent man had been railroaded by over-eager prosecutors. In August 1945, Governor Green granted a full pardon to Joe Majczek. The second convicted man was later released, and both received cash payments from the state. The killing itself was never solved. The Majczek case was later made into an acclaimed movie titled *Call Northside 777*.

October 11, 1969

The Weathermen, the most extreme faction of Students for a Democratic Society, were in Chicago to protest the Vietnam War. They began their "Days of Rage" with an October 8 window-smashing rampage through the Gold Coast. Police made 68 arrests. National Guard troops were called out, making the next two days calmer. But on October 11, violence again flared. A Loop march had been scheduled. The three hundred marchers stepped off in good order, then broke through police lines. The marchers had hidden lead pipes, hammers, railroad flares and other potential weapons in their clothing. They began throwing things at the police and smashing more windows. Order was soon restored and 105 people arrested, running the four-day total to 250. More than 50 police had been injured, as were an unknown number of Weathermen. Richard Elrod, a young assistant corporation counsel, was partially paralyzed during an encounter with one of the protesters. Elrod later became Cook County sheriff and a judge.

October 12, 1868

Marshall Field and Levi Leiter operated a dry goods store on Lake Street in 1868. Their one-time partner, Potter Palmer, was speculating in real estate. On the northeast corner of State and Washington, Palmer erected a six-story, marble-clad commercial structure. He had little trouble convincing his former associates to relocate there, even at a princely rent of $50,000 a year. Early in October, Field and Leiter began moving their stock to the new site. On October 12, a front-page ad in the *Chicago Tribune* headlined "REMOVAL AND OPENING" announced that Field, Leiter & Company had completed its move to State Street. When the doors were thrown open at 10:00 a.m., Field and Leiter were on hand to personally give each man who entered a cigar and each woman a rose. The grand new store was soon nicknamed the Marble Palace. Though that building was destroyed in the Great Fire three years later, State Street had replaced Lake as Chicago's main shopping street.

October 13, 1900

Today, a committee of Yale University faculty pronounced Chicago "the typical American city." The occasion was the Ten Eyck student essay competition, with one of the topics listed as "The American City: Chicago." The scholars felt that the problems of economic, political and social life were being solved in Chicago and that the city would be "the battleground of American civilization" in the twentieth century. Local Yale men were understandably pleased with the designation.

State Street in the early 1900s. *Author's collection.*

October 14, 1985

Early on this Monday morning, a state trooper on the Tri-State Tollway spotted a speeding and weaving Mercedes and pulled the car over. Sitting behind the wheel was Bears' head coach Mike Ditka. He'd just returned from San Francisco, where the Bears had beaten the 49ers. Now Ditka was taken to a state police station. He was charged with speeding, improper lane usage and driving under the influence of alcohol. After surrendering his driver's license and posting bond, he took a cab home. The incident soon became public news, and many football fans were angry at the police for arresting Da Coach. Secretary of State Jim Edgar was forced to issue a statement supporting the cops. A police spokesman said that Ditka had been "very polite" while in custody, and Ditka himself said that the officers were just doing their jobs. Meanwhile, the Bears announced that beer sales would be halted at halftime during the next Monday night's game against the Packers. Four months later in court, Ditka was fined $300 and had his driver's license suspended for six months. By that time, the Bears had become Super Bowl champions.

October 15, 1918

They called it Spanish flu. While World War I raged in Europe, the greatest pandemic since the Black Death raged throughout the world. The disease hit Chicago in October 1918. Influenza spread through close human contact, so health commissioner John Dill Robertson banned all large public gatherings—no sporting events, no political gatherings, no movies, no weddings, no funerals. Schools were closed and children in playgrounds sent home. Churches were allowed to stay open, since they were considered essential for morale. Most businesses continued to operate, though with staggered hours to avoid overcrowding on public transit. By the middle of the month, most of the city seemed to be wearing gauze facemasks. Yet people were dying—362 in one day alone. Then, as October moved into November, the number of deaths rapidly dropped. The war ended on November 11, and the Spanish flu was forgotten in the excitement. In Chicago, the disease had claimed 8,500 victims, including former mayor John Hopkins and pioneer educator Ella Flagg Young.

October 16, 1943

Chicago's first subway began operations on this date. The 4.9-mile-long State-Division-Clybourn tunnel had taken five years to build and cost $46 million. Though Chicago Rapid Transit was a private company, the subway had been built by the city, with some help from the federal government. The new route cut twenty minutes off travel time through the Loop. At the dedication ceremony, Mayor Kelly promised that more Chicago subways would be built once World War II was over.

October 17, 1954

Suburbs were the hot real estate in 1954. Today 1,500 people took a tour of Kenwood, an interracial Chicago neighborhood billing itself as a suburb in the city. The tours were sponsored by the Kenwood Neighborhood Redevelopment Corp., a grass-roots alliance of homeowners. Ten homes were open to the public in the area bounded by Ellis Avenue, 48th Street, Dorchester Avenue and Hyde Park Boulevard. The visitors saw a variety of adaptive reuse, including a 1901 horse barn turned into a cottage. The future looked promising to the settlers who'd stayed put rather than join the flight to the 'burbs. As one tour guide put it, Kenwood was becoming "the Lake Forest of the South Side."

October 18, 1909

Gypsy Smith really was a Romani—a gypsy. By 1909, he was a respected preacher on three continents. Smith was holding a revival in Chicago at the Wentworth Avenue armory. On this evening, after finishing his sermon, he walked out of the building and started heading up Wentworth toward the city's red-light district, the Levee. He'd announced his intention days earlier, and now the three thousand people in the congregation got up and followed him. As they moved silently through the night, Smith would occasionally turn around and preach to them while walking backward. More people joined along the way. By the time they reached 22nd Street, the crowd numbered about fifty thousand. The Levee had been alerted of Smith's march, and all the brothels were shut down with the lights off and doors locked. Periodically, the marchers would pause in front of a house to sing a hymn, then move on. The march finally ended, Smith left and the Levee cautiously reopened for business.

October 19, 1962

Chicago mayor Richard J. Daley had played an important part in helping John F. Kennedy become president. Now JFK was returning the favor, coming to Chicago to help the local Democratic ticket in the upcoming elections. The day's festivities included a presidential motorcade from O'Hare, a $100-a-plate fundraiser at McCormick Place and a giant fireworks display over the lake. More events were planned for the next day, but the president abruptly changed plans and returned to Washington. The press was told that he'd caught a cold. But a few days later, the nation learned the real reason for JFK's sudden departure—the Soviets were building secret missile bases in Cuba. It was the beginning of the Cuban Missile Crisis.

October 20, 1975

After three years and $150 million, Water Tower Place officially opened on North Michigan Avenue. The vertical shopping mall being launched today was part of a unified complex that also included a Ritz-Carlton Hotel and a seventy-four-floor high-rise with 260 condos. The mall itself had eight floors, anchored by Marshall Field's and Lord & Taylor. Chicagoans were eager to get a look at the new facility and began lining up two hours before the 10:00 a.m. opening. The first two thousand women through the doors were each given a rose. There is no record of the men getting anything.

October 21, 1926

The Hotel Sherman was the site of a gangland summit meeting convened by Al Capone today. Besides Big Al, Bugs Moran, Klondyke O'Donnell and Schemer Drucci

were among the notables attending. The assembled chieftains agreed to renounce violence as a matter of policy. Boundaries between gang territories were established, all existing feuds were called off and each leader assumed responsibility for disciplining his own people. Though peace reigned for the next few months, the Hotel Sherman Summit reinforced Chicago's unsavory image—where else did gangsters hold a press conference to announce their treaties?

The Hotel Sherman, site of the gangland peace conference. *Author's collection.*

October 22, 1930

A year after the stock market crash, the nation was beginning to feel the ripple effect. Unemployment was at 8.9 percent. Here in Chicago, the Illinois Free Employment Service was trying to find work for over a thousand men everyday. Most of the applicants were manual laborers, though many white-collar workers were showing up, saying they'd take anything offered. An alliance of social agencies called the Goodfellows Fund was collecting money to buy food, pay rent and keep utilities operating for the city's seventy-five thousand needy families. At the University of Chicago, a conference on business conditions included some forty-five leaders of the country's biggest industries and drew over one thousand members of the general public. The consensus of the conference was that the federal government should relax its hold on business. That was the best way to help the economy grow out of the current slump.

October 23, 1940

Maybe they got the idea from Atlanta, which had just staged a grand premiere for *Gone with the Wind*. The State Street Council decided Chicago should have its own Hollywood premiere and snagged the movies' greatest showman, Cecil B. DeMille. *North West Mounted Police*, De Mille's latest epic, was set in Canada and had no connection to Chicago, but that didn't matter. On the afternoon of October 23, De Mille, his stars and a contingent of movie people arrived at North Western Station. Led by horsemen dressed in Mountie uniforms, they paraded to City Hall so that Mayor Kelly could greet them. Later that evening, the Hollywood people were honored at a Palmer House banquet, where DeMille gave a speech and the stars acted out scenes from the movie. The next day saw another parade, a nationwide radio broadcast and, at last, the movie. On the third day, the troupe left town. Though *North West Mounted Police* is considered one of DeMille's lesser works, for many years afterward, Chicagoans fondly remembered the excitement of the city's first Hollywood premiere.

October 24, 1899

You might say this was the day Chicago invaded a suburb. The whole business started a year earlier, when the Lake Street Elevated Railroad wanted to extend its line west from Chicago into the village of Austin. The village was part of Cicero Township. Though most of Cicero Township didn't want the L, Austin controlled township government, and the extension was approved. So in revenge, the rest of Cicero Township hatched a plan to get rid of Austin. A petition was circulated for the City of Chicago to annex the village of Austin. When the measure went to referendum, a majority of Austin voted to stay independent. But the rest of Cicero Township voted to let Chicago take Austin, by a huge margin. That was enough to tip the outcome. Appeals to the Illinois Supreme Court failed, and on October 24, 1899, Austin became part of Chicago, as it still remains.

October 25, 1908

There had been a series of chicken thefts at the South Water Market, so when the night watchman heard the excited clucking coming from a basement, he flashed his light down the steps toward the noise. What he saw were two brown bears, calmly eating chicken. The watchman called the fire department. The firemen came, took a look down the stairs and said they only fought fires. Now, police were summoned. After surveying the situation, the cops suggested that the owner of the bears should be contacted. The owner arrived, went down into the basement and kicked the larger bear in the rump. The bear galloped up the stairs and into his cage, followed quickly by his smaller buddy. Thus the story was reported in the next day's *Tribune*, but no mention was made of what two bears were doing in the middle of a large city in the first place. Perhaps they were a common household pet in 1908.

October 26, 2005

When it finally happened, it was surprisingly easy. In 2005, the Chicago White Sox won the American League Central Division title by six games. Then they swept the Red Sox in three straight games in the Division series. Next they took the League Championship series from the Angels, four games to one. That put the Sox in the World Series against the Houston Astros—and they swept the Series in four straight. True, the last game in Houston on October 26 was a 1–0 nail-biter. But when the last out went down, a Chicago team had won the World Series for the first time in eighty-eight years.

October 27, 1956

Somebody had sabotaged Jack Muller's three-wheel motorcycle. The Chicago policeman, known as the city's champion ticket-writer, found wires pulled and switches tampered with when he retrieved his vehicle from the police garage on La Salle Street. The problem delayed Muller only slightly. Once he got rolling, he issued tickets to twenty-seven autos illegally parked around the Traffic Court building and arrested a city engineer found removing the tickets from some of the autos. Muller didn't distinguish between ordinary citizens and the ruling elite. Anybody breaking the law faced the consequences—even politicians. "What's the difference as long as the violations were observed?" he asked. Muller said he had no idea who'd vandalized his cycle, laughing, "I guess some guy couldn't wait until Halloween."

October 28, 1893

Mayor Carter Harrison. *Author's collection.*

The World's Columbian Exposition was drawing to a close. Carter Harrison, the city's popular five-term mayor, was catching an evening nap at his Ashland Boulevard residence after a busy day at the fair. About 8:00 p.m., a young man named Eugene Prendergast was allowed in to see the mayor—then shot him three times. Harrison was dead within minutes. Prendergast surrendered to police, saying he'd done the deed because Harrison refused to appoint him corporation counsel. Though Prendergast was likely insane and was defended by up-and-coming attorney Clarence Darrow, he was hanged. The city honored its martyred mayor with a statue in Union Park, with a public high school and by electing his son Carter Jr. mayor for five terms of his own.

October 29, 1955

The City of Chicago dedicated the world's largest airport on this day. Originally known as Orchard Field, it had been renamed O'Hare Airport in honor of the city's World War II flying ace, the late Edward "Butch" O'Hare. Midway Airport had no further room to expand, so in 1947, work had begun on the new airfield. Now, after eight years and $24 million, O'Hare was ready for its first commercial flight, TWA 94 to Paris. It would take eight more years and another $60 million to finish O'Hare, and the expansion and reconfiguring continues into the twenty-first century. Yet the giant air facility still retains the official airport code ORD, from its days as little Orchard Field.

October 30, 1972

Chicago's deadliest railroad accident began at 7:25 a.m., when northbound Illinois Central train no. 416 overshot the 27th Street station. The engineer stopped the train and began backing up. Three minutes behind was train no. 720, an express made up of old steel coaches. The first train had tripped a block signal when it passed the station, indicating the track was clear. Coming through the morning fog, the engineer of no. 720 saw the first train too late. The front car of no. 720 slammed into the rear of no. 416, smashing through the light-weight aluminum coaches before grinding to a halt. People screamed and tried to escape the mangled wreck. The noise of the crash brought rescue crews from nearby Michael Reese and Mercy Hospitals. Firemen arrived. Working together, they began pulling out trapped passengers—and removing the bodies of the dead. Train nos. 416 and 720 had carried a combined total of around 1,000 passengers. Of that number, 350 were injured. The final death toll was 45. As a result of the accident, the rear ends of all Chicago commuter coaches are now painted in high-visibility orange.

October 31, 1993

The Southwest Side was the last part of Chicago to get rapid transit. A 1940 plan for an Archer Avenue subway to Midway Airport never became reality. During construction of the Stevenson Expressway in the 1960s, the median strip was set aside for future transit needs. In 1980, Mayor Jane Byrne proposed building an L line using money originally earmarked for the Crosstown Expressway. Several more years passed until the needed federal funds were obtained. There were also arguments about what route the new transit line should follow. To save money, the decision was made to use existing railroad rights of way and build an elevated structure where needed. Work on the half-century-old dream finally got underway, and on October 31, 1993, the new Orange Line began service between the Loop and Midway. Provision was made to eventually extend the line to Ford City, though that has not yet been done.

November 1, 1909

On this date, a smoking ban went into effect on the trains of the Chicago & Oak Park Elevated Railroad. Since about 80 percent of adult males smoked at least one cigar a day, the new rule was unpopular. Nothing much happened the first few days, as the smokers went on smoking, and nobody stopped them. But on November 5, security guards tried to remove two smokers, other passengers stopped the guards and a near-riot ensued. Now there was a mass rally of five hundred smokers in Oak Park. A citizen's committee was formed to defend the civil right of nicotine enjoyment. Tobacco-friendly politicians threatened to revoke the L franchise, while George Plummer of the smoking group challenged the company president to settle the dispute in the boxing ring, man-to-man. Despite all the noise, the ban remained in effect, and the smokers eventually got used to it. By 1918, all Chicago L trains had gone smokeless.

November 2, 1948

This was election day 1948. At ten o'clock in the evening, the first edition of the next day's *Chicago Tribune* hit the streets with the headline "Dewey Defeats Truman." The paper was a staunch supporter of Republican presidential candidate Thomas E. Dewey, and incumbent president Harry Truman had trailed badly in all the opinion polls. First returns showed Dewey with his expected lead. Since the *Tribune* was in the middle of a printers' strike, management was in a rush to get the paper out. Over 150,000 copies were in circulation when the votes began swinging toward Truman. Later editions of the *Tribune* said that the election was "too close to call." By then, however, Truman was confirmed as the winner. Original copies of the "Dewey Defeats Truman" *Tribune* have become valued collectables, but you can purchase an inexpensive mockup of the front page at—where else?—the Truman Presidential Library.

November 3, 1936

Richard J. Daley—the original Mayor Daley—was the symbol of the Chicago Democratic Party. Yet when Daley was elected to his first political office on this date, he was running as a Republican. In 1936, the state House of Representatives was made up of three reps from each district. The two parties had an arrangement of running only two candidates in a district so that one of them would always have a minority voice. Two weeks before the 1936 election, the Republican candidate in the Ninth District died. It was too late to reprint the ballots, so the Republicans organized a write-in campaign for the "Republican" seat. Meanwhile, with the incumbent Republican dead, the Democrats felt free to run their own write-in candidate. That was thirty-four-year-old Richard J. Daley. The Republicans screamed, but there was nothing they could do about it. Daley was easily elected in the heavily Democratic district. On his first day in Springfield, Daley was sworn into office, then walked across the chamber from the Republican side to the Democrat and never looked back.

November 4, 2008

On election night 2008, an estimated 250,000 people gathered in Grant Park to celebrate the election of Barack Obama as president of the United States and to hear his victory speech. Obama was the first person of African heritage elected president. He was also the first citizen of Chicago elected to the office. Opening his seventeen-minute address with the words "Hello, Chicago!" the president-elect told the gathering, "If there is anyone out there who still doubts America is a place where all things are possible, who still wonders if the dream of our founders is alive in our time, who still questions the power of our democracy—tonight is your answer." After thanking his family, his staff and his supporters, Obama reviewed some of the themes of his campaign. He mentioned 106-year-old Ann Nixon Cooper, talking of the changes she'd seen in her long life, and closed with what he called "the timeless creed that sums up the spirit of a people—yes we can!"

November 5, 1922

The Chicago Temple. *Author's collection.*

Despite a light rain, over one thousand people gathered at the corner of Clark and Washington today to watch the cornerstone laying of the Chicago Temple. The building was to be the new home of the First Methodist Episcopal Church. A telegram from President Harding was read, and speeches were made by Mayor Thompson and a number of church dignitaries. The most amens greeted the remarks of General Charles G. Dawes. "This church stands under the shadow of the city hall, [but] I remind you that city hall stands under the shadow of this church," Dawes said. "It is the church alone that can keep us from the mob." When completed in 1924, the 568-foot Chicago Temple was the tallest building in Chicago and the tallest church in the world.

November 6, 1864

Chicago was far removed from the major battles of the Civil War. Yet this morning, the city awoke to find itself the site of a fiendish plot. Just south of the city, about ten thousand Confederate POWs were interred at Camp Douglas. According to the *Tribune*, on election day—two days from today—a force of four hundred armed men would attack the camp and free the prisoners. Then the Rebels would invade Chicago, rob the banks, burn the city to the ground and move on. Their goal was to cause enough trouble so that President Lincoln would be forced to make peace. But the *Tribune* had discovered the conspiracy just in time, and over the next few days, military authorities arrested 150 people. Nearly all of them were soon released. Only three men were convicted of anything, and some historians have asserted that the Chicago Conspiracy was merely a harebrained scheme that never had a chance of success.

November 7, 1907

Today, Chicagoans read about a club being formed by "artists, litterateurs, architects, and others with a penchant for the esthetic." The new club was to hold its meetings in a bungalow constructed on the roof of the International Harvester Building at Michigan and Harrison. Originally planned to be called the Attic Club, the ninety-five men attending the organizational meeting decided instead on the name The Cliff Dwellers. A committee headed by writer Hamlin Garland would manage the club until permanent officers were elected. Dues were set at forty dollars a year.

November 8, 1887

Early this morning, two companies of the Sixth Infantry arrived in the city from Utah on the Chicago & North Western tracks. Seven Haymarket defendants were scheduled to hang in a few days, and the city's business leaders wanted troops nearby in case of violence. The War Department had agreed to build a new fort in Highwood, twenty miles north of the city. Now, after a quick breakfast at the station, the seventy-three soldiers and seven officers reboarded their train and traveled up the North Shore to Highwood. Arriving there, they pitched their tents on the 632-acre federal tract and awaited developments. As it turned out, there would be no riots in Chicago this week. In time, the army base on the North Shore was completed. Known as Fort Sheridan, it continued in operation until 1993.

November 9, 1927

All Chicago was shocked by the brutal attack on Joe E. Lewis. The young cabaret singer had been the star attraction at the Green Mill and had recently signed to appear at the Rendezvous Lounge. Mobster Jack McGurn, one of the Green Mill owners, had warned Lewis he'd better come back. So on this morning, three strangers forced their way into Lewis's room at the Commonwealth Hotel. They took turns carving up Lewis's face and neck with a hunting knife, then left him in a pool of blood. A housemaid found the singer and got him to the hospital. Lewis lived, though his singing voice was gone, and he had to relaunch his career as a nightclub comedian. Jack McGurn, who'd ordered the attack, was killed in a bowling alley in 1936. Joe E. Lewis survived him by thirty-five years.

November 10, 1924

As a boy, Dion O'Banion had sung in the choir at Holy Name Cathedral. On this day, as a thirty-two-year-old man, he was in his florist shop across the street from the cathedral. The shop was a front for O'Banion's chief occupation: mob boss of the North Side. He was busy preparing a floral display when three men came in. O'Banion recognized the men and walked forward to greet them. While the first man shook hands with O'Banion, his two companions produced pistols and pumped six bullets into the gangster-florist. That was the end of Dion O'Banion. The assassins were thought to be members of the Capone mob, though nothing was ever proven. At O'Banion's funeral a few days later, a small basket of mixed blooms arrived. It bore the simple inscription, "From Al."

November 11, 1921

Today, Chicago was introduced to the latest method of instantaneous communication: radio. Westinghouse Electric's station KYW was broadcasting a test transmission from the stage of the Auditorium Theater. The Chicago Grand Opera Company was set to perform, with opera director Mary Garden making the introduction. Garden was supposed to say, "This is station KYW, Chicago." But the first words that went out over the air were her slightly earlier ad-lib, "My God, it's dark here!" After that, the ten-minute broadcast of orchestra music and a *Madame Butterfly* aria went off without incident. An estimated fifty thousand people listened in on their primitive crystal receivers, some from as far away as five hundred miles.

November 12, 1893

The audience at the Central Music Hall this evening was certainly diverse—"businessmen and labor leaders, representatives of city government and its executive clubs, preachers and saloon-keepers, gamblers and theological professors, matrons of distinguished families and madams from houses of ill-fame." They had been called together by visiting English editor William T. Stead for a discussion about Chicago's problems. Different speakers described the city's poverty, social neglect and political corruption. The audience asked questions, argued among themselves, cheered, booed and did some thinking. Then, Stead brought the meeting to a close. He had come to Chicago to write about the Columbian Exposition, thinking he'd left injustice behind in the Old World. "But what would Christ think of Chicago, if He should come here today?" Stead asked. "There are people in Chicago today who are not living a human life." The meeting adjourned with the audience renewed in spirit, and the city did have a powerful reform movement—for a while. Stead later published his observations on the city in a bestselling book titled *If Christ Came to Chicago.*

November 13, 1926

Royals were celebrities in 1926, and one of the biggest royal celebrities was Queen Marie of Romania. She arrived in Chicago on November 13 that year, a vivacious fifty-one-year-old lady with a scandalous past. Her three days in the city were the usual circus, with tours and banquets and speeches and a radio broadcast. The city was in awe. But though she was a queen, Marie had class, as one incident shows. When she first arrived, Marie sweetly asked the photographers not to take flash photos of her when she was walking down stairs because it blinded her and she was afraid of falling. The request was reasonable, so they honored it and thought nothing more about it. Then, at the closing banquet at the Blackstone, Marie was called on to make a toast. She stood up, raised her glass, waited to get everyone's attention and said in a ringing voice, "To the Chicago newspaper photographers!"

November 14, 1952

The *Sun-Times* inquiring reporter was asking passersby at Randolph and Michigan about the new medium, television. Would they be willing to pay a one-dollar yearly tax to ensure better TV programs? Four of the five people interviewed said they would. The one person who was against payment said the current programing was fine, so there was no need for a tax. The other four had complaints about the type of shows now on the air. Each had specific ideas on what they wanted to see—more comedy, more ballet, more football games, newer movies. Cable TV would eventually answer these concerns, but at a higher price than one dollar per year.

November 15, 1996

Back in the 1970s, the Loop seemed to be dying. After examining the situation in depth, the experts concluded that State Street was not pedestrian friendly. So in 1979, the section of State between Wacker and Congress was converted into a linear park. And from the first, there were complaints that the job hadn't been done right. The mall was broken every block by cross streets, CTA diesel buses still rumbled down the middle, the landscaping and street furniture were sterile. The State Street Mall was a hundred-foot-wide hybrid of highway and plaza, combining the worst features of both. Public feeling was, at best, lukewarm. One lady summed it up when she said, "I know that I *should* like the Mall, but I really don't." By the mid-1990s the Loop was reviving, and it made no sense to close off a major street to auto traffic. Mayor Richard M. Daley pronounced the mall dead, and old-fashioned State Street was reopened on November 15, 1996—just in time for the Christmas shopping season.

November 16, 1964

Though it was already 1964, Chicagoans were surprised to learn that the city still employed sixty-five blacksmiths. The blacksmiths had just received a $0.20 hourly raise, to $5.15 an hour. Now, Alderman John Hoellen was asking questions. The employer group that had negotiated the raise, the Blacksmith Association, was run by the vice-president of the blacksmiths' union. Hoellen said the deal was like "negotiating with yourself." Before Hoellen could delve further into what was going on, the council voted to defer the matter for further study.

November 17, 1951

A week after five Loop streets became one way, Chicagoans were having trouble adjusting. Randolph, Madison and Adams were now one way westbound, while Washington and Monroe were one way eastbound. Police reported that drivers were still sticking to the right lanes on the streets, through force of habit. Buses and taxis served passengers at the right curb, so the one-way street system had not yet resulted in faster travel through downtown. Additional one-way streets and restrictions on Loop parking were being considered as solutions to the continuing traffic jams.

November 18, 1960

Today, Chicago dedicated McCormick Place, the city's new convention hall. The "gleaming jewel of the lakefront" had taken two years to build and cost $41 million. Now it was a reality, and everything about it was big—the interior measured 1,005 feet by 300 feet, six football fields could fit on the main exhibit floor, the cafeteria could serve 1,800 people an hour and the theater had 5,081 seats. About the only complaint anyone had was that McCormick Place was ugly! The brutal concrete exterior reminded some critics of a giant mausoleum. By 1967, there was already discussion about remodeling when a timely fire destroyed the first McCormick Place.

November 19, 1905

Writer Jack London was in Chicago on a lecture tour today when his divorce was finalized in San Francisco. He immediately telegraphed Charmian Kittredge in Iowa, telling her they could now get married. While Charmian traveled to Chicago by train, Jack raced about the city trying to get the legal formalities in order—which was a problem, since it was Sunday. But after some of his previous adventures, very little could stop London. He found the license clerk, got the man to open his office and routed out a judge. At ten o'clock in the evening, Jack and Charmian "committed matrimony."

November 20, 1966

Northwestern University's female students weren't going "mod." That was the judgment of a female reporter examining the current fashions on the Evanston campus. Miniskirts, silver suits and electronic vinyl dresses were in style at many of the country's colleges. At Northwestern, almost all the young women dressed conservatively. The most common look featured turtleneck shells, blazers, skirts cut to mid-knee and nylon hose in flat shoes. Hair was secured by headbands and barrettes. Earrings were small and simple. The more daring coeds wore slacks to class, though even these were neatly pressed and coordinated with jackets.

November 21, 1953

Today's *Tribune* carried two stories from two different experts, making two predictions about the city's future. Lloyd Morey, University of Illinois acting president, said that the local Navy Pier branch had proven useful as a junior college feeder to the main campus in Urbana. Morey predicted that Chicago would have a full, four-year branch of the university by 1959. Meanwhile, in Springfield, Evan Howell of the new state toll road commission predicted that the Chicago area could have a toll highway as soon as 1956. The predictions were accurate, though both experts got the years wrong. The Northwest (Jane Addams) Tollway opened in 1958, the University of Illinois at Chicago Circle in 1965.

November 22, 1967

For Thanksgiving Eve, the Civic Opera House was presenting a jazz festival. The show was headlined by legendary saxophonist Cannonball Adderley. Guitarist Wes Montgomery and vocalist Joe Williams were also performing. The bill was rounded out by the comedy of Chitlin' Circuit veteran Moms Mabley. Two evening shows were scheduled, at 8:30 and 11:30 p.m.

November 23, 1912

The *Rouse Simmons* was the best known of the lake schooners that brought fresh evergreen trees to the Clark Street dock each Christmas season. On November 22, 1912, the ship sailed out of Thompson, Michigan. It carried five thousand trees, causing one observer to say it looked like a "floating forest." The next afternoon, one hundred miles down the Wisconsin coast, the *Rouse Simmons* was spotted flying a distress flag. A powered rescue boat was sent out to help, but heavy weather and gathering darkness made it impossible to locate the schooner. The *Rouse Simmons* had disappeared. Maritime authorities later concluded the ship had gone down in a storm. Within a few years, trains and trucks were being used to bring evergreens to Chicago. In 1971, a scuba diver finally located the sunken wreckage of the *Rouse Simmons*.

November 24, 1958

"Cop in Copter to Help Untie Traffic Knot," read the headline in the *Tribune*. Today, radio station WGN was sending a helicopter overhead to broadcast traffic reports during the afternoon rush hour. The reporter was Leonard Baldy, a thirty-one-year-old Chicago policeman. He'd be focusing on major traffic arteries such as Lake Shore Drive, Michigan Avenue and the Congress (Eisenhower) Expressway. As the weeks went by, the WGN traffic reports proved so popular they were extended to the morning rush hour and copied by other stations. Sadly, Officer Leonard Baldy was killed when his copter malfunctioned and crashed on May 2, 1960.

November 25, 1910

Mary Garden as "Salome." *Author's collection.*

Salome was the latest opera from the German composer Richard Strauss. The work had scandalized Europe—the music was too discordant, the dancing too erotic, everything about it too "modern." Naturally, it had played to sold-out houses. Now the opening night of the Chicago production, starring soprano Mary Garden, drew the usual Social Register crowd. The next day's papers were full of *Salome*. A few people called Strauss's work a masterpiece; many more called it obscene. Police Chief Roy Steward attended the performance and was shocked. He said that Mary Garden's dancing was disgusting, that she "wallowed around like a cat on a bed of catnip." The debate flashed back and forth for the rest of *Salome*'s Chicago run. The notorious opera eventually became part of the standard repertoire, and Richard Strauss made enough money from it to build a vacation villa.

November 26, 1833

On this date, the three hundred residents of Chicago got their first newspaper. The publisher was John Calhoun, a printer who'd run a string of failed papers in upstate New York and was trying his luck in a new place. Calhoun's latest venture was a weekly called the *Chicago Democrat*. Like most papers of the era, he filled his columns by copying news from out-of-town publications. The one original piece of work in the first issue was an editorial coming out boldly in favor of a canal or railroad to link Lake Michigan and the Mississippi River. In our time, Chicago's first newspaper mogul is memorialized in Calhoun Place, an alley between Madison and Washington in the Loop.

November 27, 1937

What's the record for the largest crowd to attend an American football game? The answer is 120,000, on this date at Soldier Field. And it was a high school game! Austin of the Public League was meeting Leo of the Catholic League in Mayor Ed Kelly's Prep Bowl. Tickets sold for one dollar each at firehouses, though your precinct captain could probably get you one for free. Billy DeCorrevont of Austin was the running back wiz of the Public League, and it seemed the whole city wanted to see how he'd do against Leo's iron defense. The fans came, sat in aisles or stood on anything solid. DeCorrevont added to his press clippings by scoring three touchdowns and passing for a fourth as Austin beat Leo, 30–6. As for that attendance, nobody really knows how many people squeezed into Soldier Field that day. Chicago police estimated 115,000. Usher boss Andy Frain said 125,000. The 120,000 figure has been accepted as a compromise.

Soldier Field in the 1930s. *Author's collection.*

November 28, 1895

America's first automobile race took place on this date—right through the streets of Chicago. The *Chicago Times-Herald* sponsored the Thanksgiving Day event, offering a first prize of $2,000 and a gold medal. At 8:55 a.m., with about two thousand people watching, the six cars roared out of Jackson Park at a break-neck twelve miles per hour. They moved along the city's boulevards, through downtown and up toward Evanston. More spectators had gathered along the route, and policemen on horseback rode ahead to clear the way. By afternoon, when the cars turned around to head south, only three were still running. Back in Chicago, leader Frank Duryea misread a direction sign and turned down the wrong street. He finally got back on course, only to be stopped at a railroad crossing as a freight train slowly rumbled through. At 7:30 p.m., Duryea finally crept through the darkness at the Jackson Park finish line. Only then did he learn that he was the winner of the fifty-four-mile long "Chicago Grand Prix."

November 29, 1959

The Chicago Cardinals had been a founding member of the National Football League. Though the team won NFL championships in 1925 and 1947, by 1959 Chicago had become a Bears town. Now the Cardinals were at Soldier Field, playing their final home game of the year against their crosstown rivals. Rumors were already spreading that the franchise would be transferred out of Chicago, and a standing-room-only crowd of forty-nine thousand braved the twenty-degree chill to witness what might be the Big Red's farewell performance. Could the last-place Cardinals reward their fans with an upset victory over the mighty Bears? Great idea for a fairytale, but not for real life. The Cardinals lost, 31–7. The team then went on the road for their last two games and lost those, too. By the time the 1960 season rolled around, the Cardinals had moved to St. Louis.

November 30, 1923

Five hundred women came to Chicago today for a conference of the National Women's Rights Party. They met at the Rush Street mansion of Ganna Walska, an aspiring opera singer married to industrialist Harold McCormick. At the meeting, speakers detailed how women were treated as second-class citizens. Under common law tradition, a husband had complete control of all the couple's assets—he could even force his wife to work, then keep the money for himself. A woman aspiring to a career on her own ran into state laws that prohibited her from working in certain jobs. Recalling the landmark Seneca Falls Convention of 1848, another speaker predicted it could take another seventy-five years for women to achieve full equality. The best solution might be to add an equal rights amendment to the U.S. Constitution. With the delegates determined to continue the fight, the conference adjourned.

December 1, 1958

Our Lady of the Angels School in the Humboldt Park neighborhood had about 1,300 students. On this date, sometime after 2:00 p.m., a fire started in a waste barrel near the bottom of a stairwell. The building had no sprinklers, only two fire alarms and limited exits. By the time the fire was discovered, it could not be contained. Some teachers were able to lead their classes to safety. Others weren't so fortunate, as the corridors were soon jammed with panicked students. Many kids tried to escape by jumping out windows. Firemen arrived and performed heroically. But the final death toll was ninety-five—ninety-two students and three nuns. Our Lady of the Angels was the worst-ever school fire in Chicago and one of the deadliest in American history.

December 2, 1942

World War II was on, and the United States was in a race with Nazi Germany to develop an atomic bomb. Enrico Fermi's team of physicists was working on the secret project at the University of Chicago's Metallurgical Laboratory. Their goal was to develop a self-sustaining nuclear pile. Since their new lab in suburban Argonne wasn't ready, they carried on their experiments in a room under the grandstand at Stagg Field, the university's unused football stadium. On the afternoon of December 2, the team was ready to test the nuclear pile. Nobody knew what would happen if the experiment got out of control. There might be an explosion or massive radiation leaks. The test lasted a tense four and a half minutes. Fermi checked the numbers, concluded that the nuclear pile worked and ended the procedure. Everyone exhaled. The atomic age had been born.

December 3, 1943

In 1943, Ric Riccardo and Ike Sewell wanted to start a Mexican restaurant. But after they tried preparing some Mexican food, they decided to go with their second choice, pizza. The two men rented the basement of an old town house across from Medinah Temple. Then some genius—and there's still argument whether it was Riccardo, Sewell or someone else—came up with "The Idea." Pizza had always been served in tiny wedges with a thin crust. Why not cook it in a deep dish, with heaps of cheese and tomato? On the evening of December 3, Pizzeria Uno opened with little fanfare. Business was slow at first, then gradually caught on. Since that modest debut in 1943, Chicago-style pizza has spread around the globe.

Pizzeria Uno, where deep-dish pizza was born. *Photo by the author.*

December 4, 1921

It began in October, when the *Herald-Examiner* ran a story about a visiting millionaire who was passing out money to people, just to see them smile. Shortly afterward, the *H-E* started printing smile coupons in the paper, with one lucky coupon cutter winning $1,000 in a weekly raffle. Over at the *Tribune*, the bosses thought the whole thing was just a stunt to boost circulation. But the *H-E* was selling more papers now, and the *Tribune* couldn't be left behind. In November, the *Tribune* launched its own giveaway, Cheer Checks. The *H-E* responded by raising its prizes, the *Tribune* re-raised, and so on. By December, daily prizes had reached $7,000, with the special Sunday drawing worth $20,000. Now people were buying armloads of papers, ripping out the coupons and tossing the rest into the street. Fights broke out among customers at newsstands. Finally, on December 4, the postmaster general asked both papers to stop their smile raffles. That ended the competition. Going forward, Chicagoans would have to find their own reason to crack a smile.

December 5, 1901

One of Chicago's most famous sons is not often thought of as a Chicagoan. Walt Disney was born in a house that still stands on the Northwest Side on December 5, 1901. His father, Elias, had come to the city in 1890 to work as a carpenter at the Columbian Exposition, then stayed on once the fair ended. In 1893, Elias built the two-story frame house in the Hermosa neighborhood, got other carpentry jobs and became a trustee in the nearby Congregational church. Walt was the family's fourth son. In 1906, the Disneys moved to a farm in Missouri. But in 1917, after living in various places and trying different occupations, Elias Disney brought them back to Chicago. The new home was on the near West Side, where Walt attended classes at McKinley High School. Walt drew cartoons for the school paper and took art classes at night, leaving after one year to become an ambulance driver in World War I. He never again lived in Chicago.

December 6, 1866

In search of cleaner drinking water, the city council approved constructing a tunnel out into Lake Michigan in 1864. A new intake crib was built two miles from shore and then the digging of the tunnel began, moving from both sides to the middle. Each end had two crews working twelve-hour shifts, six days a week. Two shovel men led the way, followed by masons who laid brick around the walls for support. Rail cars pulled by mules removed the debris. The 10,587-foot-long tunnel was completed on December 6, 1866, at a final cost of $380,784. The Chicago Tunnel was the first water supply tunnel to an American city. Water started flowing the following March, when the pumping station on Michigan Avenue was finished.

December 7, 1941

The news hit Chicago shortly after noon. The Japanese had attacked Pearl Harbor in Hawaii, and the United States was suddenly thrust into World War II. And just as suddenly, all Chicago was in motion. The city's six railroad terminals and Municipal Airport were jammed with travelers whose plans had abruptly changed. People hauled out American flags and hung them on porches. Neighbors who hadn't spoken in years exchanged greetings. Newspapers hit the streets with extra editions. On Madison Street, four windows were smashed at the Oriental Trading Company, though no other violence against local Japanese was reported. Already, lines were forming at military recruiting offices. At the Warren Avenue police station, an army deserter from Texas turned himself in, saying, "I want to go back and do my part." Chicago was at war. It would not know peace for 1,351 days.

December 8, 1902

Today, the city council passed an ordinance requiring all automobiles to display numbers. The rear of the vehicle must have numbers at least eight inches high, of such color as to be easily distinguished. The autos were also ordered to display numbers on the front and side lamps that could be read at a distance of seventy-five feet. Failure to obey the ordinance resulted in a maximum fine of fifty dollars for each day of violation. Similar laws were already on the books in Boston and other cities. An automobile driver had caused a recent accident on Michigan Avenue, then fled the scene without being identified, and police were still searching for the reckless driver.

December 9, 1889

In 1886, arts patron Ferdinand Peck organized a syndicate to give Chicago a grand opera hall. Opera usually operated in the red, so the plan was to put the hall in a larger commercial building, which would produce enough profits to balance the budget. The ten-story Auditorium took three years to build and filled an entire block along Congress Street. When completed, it included a hotel, stores and offices—as well as the 4,200-seat opera hall—making it the largest building in the country. On December 9, 1889, the Auditorium was dedicated by President Benjamin Harrison. Saved from demolition in later years, the Auditorium eventually became the home of Roosevelt University.

The Auditorium. *Author's collection.*

December 10, 1929

On this date, the circuit court killed plans to erect the tallest building in Chicago. John F. Cuneo wanted to put a sixty-story, 667-foot office tower on the northeast corner of Michigan and Randolph. The zoning board had obligingly granted a waiver from the law requiring specific setbacks on tall buildings. Now, Judge Thomas Taylor's seventy-five-thousand-word ruling said that the waiver amounted to special legislation and revoked the Cuneo Tower's building permit. The state supreme court later affirmed the circuit court's decision. The Cuneo Tower was never built.

December 11, 1921

Tommy O'Connor was a young Maxwell Street punk who'd killed a policeman. He was in custody at the old county jail, scheduled to be hanged on December 15, 1921. But four days before that, he got ahold of a pistol. Along with four other prisoners, O'Connor managed to subdue five guards and five trusties, then escape onto the street. Two guards rushed out of the building just in time to see O'Connor jump on the running board of a passing car and force the driver at gunpoint to high-tail it away. The four other escapees were soon recaptured; Tommy O'Connor was never seen again. In the years to come, stories circulated that Terrible Tommy had gone to Ireland to fight for the IRA or that he'd repented and become a Trappist monk. In the meantime, since he had been sentenced to be "hanged by the neck until dead," the gallows was saved. When the new county jail was built, the gallows was moved there. In 1977, officials concluded that they weren't likely to run into O'Connor again, so the macabre keepsake was finally sold.

December 12, 1965

Rookie halfback Gale Sayers of the Bears scored six touchdowns against the 49ers at Wrigley Field today, tying the NFL record for a single game. His TDs were—(1) eighty-yard reception of a screen pass, (2) twenty-one-yard run from scrimmage, (3) seven-yard run from scrimmage, (4) fifty-yard run from scrimmage, (5) one-yard plunge and (6) eighty-five-yard punt return. Sayers's feat was all the more remarkable because the field was muddy after a hard morning rain. Bears head coach George Halas said, "I never saw such a thing in my life—it was the greatest performance ever by one man on a football field."

December 13, 2008

Illinois governor Rod Blagojevich had been arrested by federal agents. He was charged with corrupt practices in office, including trying to sell the U.S. Senate seat vacated by president-elect Obama. Now reporters descended on the governor's Albany Park home to hear what he had to say and to see what would happen next. The vigil would continue through his impeachment, removal from office, two trials and finally end on March 15, 2012, when Blagojevich became the fourth of the last eight Illinois governors—and the second in a row—to wind up behind bars.

December 14, 1908

Bathhouse John Coughlin and Hinky-Dink Michael Kenna were aldermen from Chicago's notorious First Ward. Each year they staged a fundraiser at the Coliseum called the First Ward Ball. By 1908, many of the city's "best" people were attending, along with the usual crew of gamblers and pickpockets and prostitutes. When the ball got underway on December 14, about twenty thousand revelers were on hand. The next day's *Tribune* reported that ten thousand quarts of champagne and thirty thousand quarts of beer had been consumed. The paper also told about the toughs trying to undress unescorted young ladies, the men wearing women's costumes, the topless hookers, the fistfights and the one stabbing with a hatpin. Even for easygoing Mayor Fred Busse this was too much, and he refused to give Coughlin and Kenna another liquor license. That ended the First Ward Ball.

The Chicago Coliseum, around the time of the First Ward Ball. *Author's collection.*

December 15, 1955

Daniel Burnham's 1909 Plan of Chicago had called for a wide parkway extending west from downtown along Congress Street. Burnham was a visionary, but it's not likely he envisioned the modern "superhighway" dedicated on December 15, 1955. The Congress Expressway had taken three years to build, cost $185 million and required the demolition of over one thousand buildings, as well as the relocation of three thousand bodies from two cemeteries. Though a couple other expressways were already in place on Chicago's outskirts, the Congress was the first one that cut through the heart of the city to downtown. Today's four-and-a-half-mile-long section between Ashland and Laramie opened with little ceremony, since everyone was anxious to try out the new road at forty-five miles per hour. The other pieces of the Congress Expressway were completed in 1960. Four years after that, it was renamed the Eisenhower—making it Chicago's only Republican expressway.

December 16, 1903

Today, Chicagoans were learning all about Mickey Finn. Mickey owned the Lone Star Saloon & Palm Garden on South State Street. One of his barmaids, Gold Tooth Mary Thornton, was telling a special city commission how the business operated. A sign in the tavern suggested patrons "Try a Mickey Finn Special." The sign didn't reveal that the special was a mixture of raw alcohol, snuff-soaked water and a white liquid supplied by a voodoo doctor. Anyone who drank the cocktail was knocked out cold. The victim was then dragged into a backroom, where Mickey would rifle his pockets, then dump him in the back alley. According to Gold Tooth Mary, her boss had no fear of the police because he was friends with Alderman Kenna, and he always saved the best cigars for the local cops. This time, however, all the bad publicity forced city officials to revoke the Lone Star's liquor license. Mickey left town and added to his fortune by selling his secret formula to other saloonkeepers. In tribute to the inventor, any kind of knockout drink has become known as a Mickey Finn.

December 17, 1931

The city was going broke, the schools were a mess, unemployment was rising and crime was everywhere. But today, in the Chicago City Council, the aldermen were holding hearings on what women could wear at the beach. Yes, the old Victorian standards were out of date. Society was changing. Alderman Thomas Grady of the Fourteenth Ward chaired the hearings, declaring that the council should adopt "modern specifications for proper swimming costumes." In the past, a woman on a public beach was expected to wear long black stockings, full-bloomers and a long-sleeve blouse—or risk arrest for public indecency. Various prominent women gave their opinions on the new swimwear, though the fifty male members of the council would ultimately decide the matter. The *Tribune* wryly suggested that "several models appear wearing the newest suits at the aldermanic meeting," running a front-page photo of four aldermen admiring a young lady in a backless suit. In the end, official approval was given to modern swimsuits, and the council was free to move on to other business.

December 18, 1932

The 1932 National Football League season had ended in a first-place tie between the Chicago Bears and the Spartans of Portsmouth, Ohio. That meant a playoff game for the championship at Wrigley Field on Sunday, December 18. As game-day approached, the weather forecast promised single-digit temperatures. Rather than lose money and be embarrassed playing before empty stands, NFL officials switched the game to the Chicago Stadium. The cramped, indoor venue caused some temporary rule adjustments, such as starting each scrimmage play from the center of the field and moving the goal posts forward to the goal line. Despite the harsh weather, a crowd of 11,193 came out—or rather, came in—to watch the Bears defeat the Spartans, 9–0. Afterward, the NFL decided that some of the temporary indoor rules made an action-packed game, so those rules became permanent. The league itself was divided into two conferences. Now each season would climax with the excitement of a championship game.

December 19, 1997

Today, Chicago native Janet Jagan was sworn in as president of Guyana. Born in 1920, she'd grown up as Janet Rosenberg on the West Side. In 1943, she married dentistry student Cheddi Jagan and moved with him to his native land, then a colony known as British Guiana. There, they became active in the independence movement, continuing in politics after independence was achieved. Cheddi was elected president in 1992. After his death early in 1997, Janet became a candidate for the office and won. The "Evita from Chicago" served until 1999, when she resigned for health reasons.

December 20, 1976

After twenty-one years in office, Mayor Richard J. Daley died today of an apparent heart attack. The seventy-four-year-old Daley had been troubled by chest pains over the weekend. Now, on Monday afternoon, he'd gone to his doctor's office at 900 North Michigan Avenue. During the exam, Daley collapsed. Paramedics were called. They worked on the mayor, but at 3:50 p.m., he was pronounced dead. Over the next few days, the city grieved, like a child suddenly orphaned. Daley's all-night wake at Nativity of Our Lord Church drew more than 100,000 people. President-elect Jimmy Carter, Vice President Nelson Rockefeller, Senator Edward Kennedy and other men of power came to the funeral. Afterward, a concerned ten-year-old boy was said to have asked his father, "Who's going to be the mayordaley now?" But though one man had died, Chicago lived on—and eventually got a mayordaley named Daley.

December 21, 1910

In 1836, when Chicago was still a village, the commissioners building the Illinois & Michigan Canal made the lakefront public land. They ruled that it would be "a common to remain forever open, clear, and free of any buildings, or any obstruction whatsoever." At the time, the lake came up to Michigan Avenue. Though the law seemed clear, that didn't stop attempts to get around it. In 1856, the Illinois Central built a railroad trestle through the site. Later the city started dumping debris into the area between the tracks and Michigan. The landfill was soon crowded with squatters' shacks among the mounds of refuse. By 1890, mail-order tycoon Montgomery Ward had enough. He brought suit to have the lakefront cleared and kept open. Over the next twenty years, he continued the fight. Finally, and definitively, the Illinois Supreme Court upheld Ward's action on December 21, 1910. Over a century later, Montgomery Ward is celebrated as the man who saved the lakefront for the people of Chicago.

December 22, 1978

Police were questioning contractor John Gacy about the disappearance of a Des Plaines teenager. They began searching the crawl space of his Norwood Township home and found human remains. Now, Gacy confessed. He'd killed the Des Plaines teenager and perhaps thirty more young men since 1972. Over the next several weeks, the bodies of twenty-nine victims were recovered from the crawl space and another four from the Des Plaines River. Gacy was indicted on thirty-three counts of murder in 1980. He was found guilty on all thirty-three counts and executed in 1994.

December 23, 1879

The first seven columns on the front page of today's *Chicago Daily News* were devoted to a bank official who'd absconded to Germany. Of greater lasting significance was the short piece in column eight. Thomas Edison had perfected his electric light bulb. "It is reported that he will light up all the houses and street lamps in Menlo Park, and publicly demonstrated that he can do all he claims," the story said. "It will not only illuminate things, but it will rock a cradle, run a sewing machine, and do light house work." Edison himself predicted that the day of cheap, reliable energy had arrived. "We will send light all night and power all day," the inventor said. "I have a little motor with which I have been raising five gallons of water fifty feet high every minute." Meanwhile, at the Montreal Stock Exchange, the price of a share in one gas company fell five points.

December 24, 1964

With the Christmas Eve rush upon them, Chicago-area transportation companies were reporting record business. The Greyhound Bus Company said that traffic was up nearly 15 percent from last year, so it was calling all available employees back to work. The Illinois Central Railroad had added twenty-one extra trains, while the Chicago & North Western's coaches were packed with thousands of sailors returning home from Great Lakes Naval Training Center. The Santa Fe Railroad was so full it was suspending local ticket sales until after the New Year. At O'Hare Airport, both American Airlines and TWA were scheduling additional flights. United Airlines was also busy. A United spokesman said the airline would probably set a new one-day passenger record today—and then break it on January 4, when holiday travelers made their return trips.

December 25, 1865

Stockyards are places where animals are slaughtered so they can be turned into table meat. During the 1850s, as Chicago developed into a railroad center, it became the final destination for the cattle that the cowboys were

driving to Dodge City, Abilene, Wichita and all those other wild towns that used to be featured in western movies. Many small stockyards sprang up in various parts of the city. Logistically, it made more sense to put all operations in one place. In 1865, some of the Chicago railroads got together, purchased land near Halsted and 39th Streets, and established the Union Stock Yards. The first shipment of hogs happened to arrive on Christmas Day, so that was the official opening of the facility. At their peak, the yards processed more that 15 million animals a year. Changes in the meatpacking industry eventually made the big yards in Chicago obsolete, and they closed in 1971.

Chicago's Union Stock Yards.
Author's collection.

December 26, 1916

Years before 9-1-1, telephone operators were dealing with emergency calls. "Phone girl" Margaret Carney's story was on the front page of today's *Tribune*. She had taken a call from a woman who'd started giving a phone number and then fainted. Carney traced the caller as Mrs. Amelia Oster of Kedzie Avenue. Carney phoned a next-door neighbor, telling the neighbor to bring a doctor to Mrs. Oster's apartment. After that, Carney was able to figure out that Mrs. Oster had been trying to phone her son. Carney called the son, who rushed over to Kedzie Avenue. There, he met the neighbor and a doctor. Because of Margaret Carney's fast thinking, the doctor had arrived in time to save Mrs. Oster's life.

December 27, 1905

The state had outlawed gambling, so the Washington Park Club and Racetrack was going out of business. The property near 61st and Cottage Grove would likely bring over $1 million when sold to developers. Club members had been sent notices to clear their belongings from the clubhouse. The Gentlemen's Driving Club, which had used the track for its Sunday afternoon entertainments, would probably relocate to the racetrack in Wheaton.

December 28, 1951

Janet Ayer Fairbank could have led a life like many of her blue-blood Gold Coast peers in the first half of the twentieth century. She did perform all the Social Register duties, serving on charity boards and the like. Yet she was much more. Fairbank had talent as a writer, turning out seven novels, a play and numerous short stories. She championed women's rights, once advertising the cause by charging down Michigan Avenue on a white horse. Most notably, she became a political player. In 1912, Fairbank was part of Theodore Roosevelt's Progressive Party campaign for president. Later, she moved over to the Democrats, helped Judge William E. Dever become Chicago's mayor and served a term as the party's national committeewoman from Illinois. Each New Year's Day, Janet and her husband, Kellogg Fairbank, gave an all-day reception at their town house that attracted hundreds of people from society, the arts, social causes and politics—a diverse cast that reflected the many interests of the hostess. Janet Ayer Fairbank died on December 28, 1951. A few days later, the final reception at 1244 North State Street became her memorial service.

December 29, 1923

Some 160 Chicagoans received New Year's greetings from Leo Koretz. The cards were inscribed with verse: "If I could be transported/ This moment to your door/ I'd bring you smiles by dozens/ And good wishes by the score/—Leo Koretz." Those 160 people certainly knew Leo Koretz. He'd conned them into investing $10 million in a bogus oil development in Panama, then disappeared with the money. So where was Leo now? The cards had been mailed in Chicago. As it turned out, he was in Nova Scotia, living it up with assorted women. Koretz was extradited, convicted of his swindle and sentenced to state prison. He told reporters he'd never serve his time. Before he could be transferred from the county lockup, one of his lady friends brought him a five-pound box of chocolate. Koretz ate it in one sitting and keeled over dead, as he'd planned. He was a diabetic.

December 30, 1903

The Iroquois Theatre opened in the fall of 1903. Located on Randolph just west of State, it was a modern 1,700-seat playhouse that proudly advertised itself as "absolutely fireproof." On this Wednesday afternoon, a packed house of mostly women and children were chuckling over the musical comedy *Mr. Bluebeard*, starring Eddie Foy. Midway into the second act, a defective lamp set a backstage curtain on fire. At first, the audience thought the glow coming from behind the stage was part of the show. Then, they started getting restless. On stage, Eddie Foy tried to calm them. When a piece of burning debris fell, someone screamed. The crowd rushed for the exits. They found the balcony doors locked. On the ground floor the doors opened inward, causing a panicked pile-up. With the situation beyond him, Foy turned his attention to his troupe and got them safely out of the building. But 602 people died. The Iroquois Theatre tragedy claimed more than twice as many victims as the Great Fire of 1871 and led to a revision of Chicago's fire laws.

December 31, 1999

Like many people in other places, many Chicagoans spent this day worrying about Y2K. "Y2K" was short for year 2000, and the problem was with computers. Programmers had been rendering years with only the last two digits. Now, there was concern that those computers wouldn't know what to do when the year clicked over from "99" to "00." Anything electronic might go crazy! So there had been feverish attempts to correct the glitch. Chicago businesses had coughed up over $2 billion for upgrades. Motorola was the biggest spender, at $230 million, followed by Abbott Labs, at $100 million. The city's Department of Children and Family Services said they could have used the money they'd spent to hire 186 more caseworkers. When midnight arrived, however, nothing much happened. Computer programmers breathed a sigh of relief. Then they started preparing for Y3K.

ABOUT THE AUTHOR

John R. Schmidt is a fifth-generation Chicagoan. He earned his PhD in history at the University of Chicago and has taught at all levels, from kindergarten through college, including over thirty years in the Chicago Public School system. Besides his earlier book, *The Mayor Who Cleaned Up Chicago*, he has published over three hundred articles in magazines, newspapers, encyclopedias and anthologies.

Schmidt has been a senior writer at *Bowlers Journal* since 1990. He is also a regular on-air contributor at radio station WBEZ and proprietor of the blog Chicago History Today.